Napoleon III and the Second Empire

PROBLEMS IN EUROPEAN CIVILIZATION

Under the editorial direction of
John Ratté
Amherst College

Napoleon III and the Second Empire

Second Edition

Edited and with an introduction by

Samuel M. Osgood

Kent State University

D. C. HEATH AND COMPANY
Lexington, Massachusetts Toronto London

CONTENTS

INTRODUCTION

Early in 1962, the following entry appeared in the "In Memoriam" column of the London *Times:*

H. M. the Emperor Napoleon III

> In respectful memory of a beneficent and far-sighted man, died January 9, 1873. He has found peace; one day he will find true justice.
> The Hon. Secretary of the Souvenir Napoléonien, in England.[1]

The existence of a society of the "Souvenir Napoléonien" in that very same England where a generation of children went to sleep in fear that "Boney" would haunt their dreams indicates that the Napoleonic legend is being perpetuated in the strangest places. Coming after some forty years of extensive new research and "revisionism," the Society's expressed hope that the nephew might yet find true justice serves as a reminder that the historians' verdict on Napoleon III is still far from conclusive or unanimous.

To be sure, historians seldom reach a unanimous or conclusive verdict on any given phase of history. They can be counted upon, however, invariably to disagree when it comes to the interpretation of developments in Modern France. How else could it be! Since the Great Revolution of 1789 (an earthshaking event over which blood and ink have been spilled in seemingly equal proportion), France has been governed by five Republics, two types of Monarchy, two Empires, and the Vichy regime of World War II which belongs in a class by itself. In the process, innumerable heroes, martyrs, and villains have been involved in an endless series of revolutions, uprisings, plots, coups, "days," affairs, scandals, and wars. France has been and con-

[1] Quoted from Genêt, "Letter From Paris," *The New Yorker,* January 20, 1962.

tinues to be a case study in political permutation; or a laboratory for institutional and constitutional experimentation. The country's strategic location and its important cultural and intellectual contributions to Western Civilization, as well as the mystique of France as the universal fatherland of man, have served further to incite the interest of historians—both at home and abroad. All this has resulted in the compilation of one of the most voluminous, controversial, and controverted historiographies on record.

In this vast body of historical literature, Napoleon III and the Second Empire occupy a special place. The man, the problems of the times, and the nature of the regime add up to a complex field of inquiry. They confront the historian with difficult questions, and are open to a variety of interpretations. Here also, then, are to be found all the ingredients for historical speculation and debate.

First, there was the man himself, the heir to the Napoleonic legend. What kind of man was Louis-Napoleon Bonaparte? For that matter, was he even entitled to the name? Whether or not he was actually the son of Napoleon's brother Louis, the former King of Holland, is not very important. The number of pages devoted by historians to the question of his paternity is merely symbolic of the aura of enigma which continues to surround the person of Napoleon III. Even today, with a century's perspective, only one thing is certain: there was nothing simple about the man. In the words of Albert Guérard, certainly one of the Emperor's ablest and staunchest champions: "To the present day no scrupulous historian can draw a clear-cut portrait of him and say with assurance, 'This is the authentic Napoleon III.' "[2]

The most superficial account of Louis-Napoleon's career immediately brings out the complexities of his personality. If his histrionic attempts to seize power in 1836 and 1840 can be dismissed as the senseless undertakings of a mad adventurer, the solitary years of study during his long captivity at the fortress (he himself called it his "University") of Ham show application and single-mindedness. To his babbling debut as a backbencher in the Constituent Assembly must be contrasted the consummate political machinations of the President and Emperor. His uncontested personal charm, kindness, and politeness were matched on occasion by the ruthlessness of an

2 Albert Guérard, *France: A Modern History* (Ann Arbor, 1959), p. 304.

autocrat. His undeniable dreams of glory were offset by an instinctive revulsion to the horrors of war. The self-indulgence of an indefatigable Don Juan, the mental and physical torpitude at the end of his reign, gave way to the resignation and dignity of the last years in exile.

And always in the background, casting its lengthy shadow over the man, his words, his actions (and his innermost thoughts?), was the colossal figure of the Little Corporal. The legend which proved such an asset to Louis-Napoleon in his quest for power turned into a liability once his ambitions had been realized. For the inevitably unfavorable comparisons began with his election to the Presidency on December 10, 1848. How many political figures, not excluding former Presidents of the United States, would attest to the fact that one of history's meanest tricks is to place a man in the position of having to compete with a legend! Few of the older dynasties number even one Napoleon in their ranks. The problem is compounded when the dynasty's founder, and the heir's sole predecessor, happens to be a Napoleon.

Small wonder, then, that Napoleon III's first critics should judge him, not in his own right, but in the light of the carefully contrived image of his famous uncle. Thus, Victor Hugo used the unlimited talents at his disposal to draw a scathing picture of "Napoleon the Little." And Karl Marx was prompt to remind us that if all great personalities reappear upon the stage of history, "on the first occasion, they appear as tragedy; on the second as farce." It is not given to many statesmen to number among their contemporaries, critics of Victor Hugo's and Karl Marx's stature. There is no evidence that Napoleon III derived any consolation from this dubious privilege. More important, the damage to his reputation was long-lasting. Theodore Zeldin, a recent English student of the Second Empire whose views are expressed in the article "The Myth of Napoleon III," has aptly remarked: "It is time that the abuse of his enemies should be appreciated in its true light, and not accepted as impartial history merely because they happened to be distinguished men." Portions of *Napoleon the Little* and *The Eighteenth Brumaire of Louis-Bonaparte* are presented here not as examples of impartial history (if there be such a thing), but as influential starting points in the historical debate over Napoleon III. In any event, as shall be seen, the Victor Hugo–Karl Marx school still has its adherents.

That all of the Emperor's contemporaries did not concur with the estimates of these detractors, is clearly shown in the passages selected from J. P. Gooch's *The Second Empire*. Today, moreover, the defenders of Napoleon III, especially in England and America, far outnumber his critics. While varying in their ultimate estimates of the man, F. A. Simpson, Albert Guérard, Hendrick Boon, and Theodore Zeldin all give due justice to his personal and statesmanlike qualities. Yet Adrien Dansette, the latest French student of the question, gives a much more qualified estimate. And J. M. Thompson, another modern scholar, who compares Napoleon III to Hamlet, "a man too small for the great things he set out to do," is most reluctant to reach a verdict. Finally, with Henri Guillemin and A. F. Thompson we return to highly critical portraits, reminiscent of Victor Hugo's opinion of the man.

The ultimate evaluation of a historical figure's performance must take his health into consideration. This is especially important in the case of a chief executive who wields as much personal power as did Napoleon III. Neither friend nor foe would contest the fact that he suffered from a variety of ailments throughout his reign. To what extent did his illnesses "affect his political decisions and his ability to govern?" This is the question to which Roger L. Williams addresses himself in a pioneering study based on a thorough analysis of the Emperor's medical record.

Second, there were the times. The years 1848–1871 were crucial ones for France—in terms both of domestic and of international developments. At home, the chronic political illness had taken a turn for the worse with the overthrow of the July Monarchy. Here one central, formidable, and unavoidable question confronts the historian: Was the Revolution of 1848 the one unnecessary upheaval? Or, to put it another way, why should France cast off the relatively benevolent regime of Louis-Philippe merely and meekly to surrender herself to the man on horseback? Even when viewed within the limited scope of our immediate interest (*i.e.* as providing Louis-Napoleon with a sudden and unexpected opportunity), the events of 1848–1852 are open to a variety of interpretations. If F. A. Simpson makes a solid case against the long-standing verdict that Louis-Napoleon's election to the Presidency in December, 1848, was due to his name alone, the deep-rooted causes of his advent to power

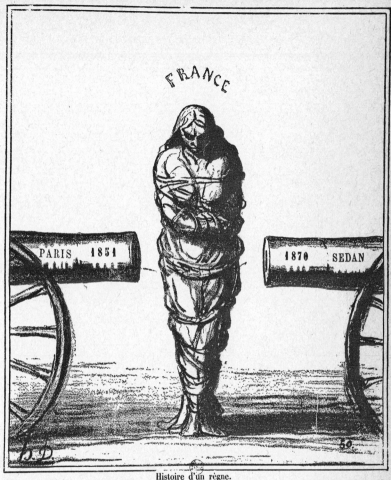

Histoire d'un règne.

FIGURE 1. If a picture is worth a thousand words, this scathing indictment of the Second Empire by Honoré Daumier did more to damage Napoleon III's reputation than the outpourings of a Marx or a Hugo. *(Photo. Bibl. nat. Paris)*

remain the object of a lively controversy. Did his election to the Presidency, the Coup of December 2, 1851, and the founding of the Second Empire a year later, constitute an inexorable sequence of events, explainable in the light of dialectic materialism as Marx would have us believe? Was Louis-Napoleon brought to power by a scheming bourgeoisie, scared out of its wits by the June Days, and ready to surrender its liberty for the sake of preserving its property? This last thesis is the one defended by Henri Guillemin.

The second half of the 19th century also witnessed important economic and social changes in France. If the pace was perhaps not quick enough to speak of an Industrial Revolution, a long step was nevertheless taken toward her transformation into a modern country. The Emperor, whose advanced views were to earn him the label "Saint-Simon on horseback," was certainly a man of his times, intent on promoting and directing the expansion of the French economy. It is undeniable that there was much progress and prosperity under the Second Empire. Whether this progress and prosperity occurred because or in spite of Napoleon III's policies is another question to which the student will find a variety of answers in the texts which form the body of this book.

On the social scene a new element was introduced with the appearance of a rapidly growing proletariat. Although he called himself a socialist, Louis-Napoleon was never willing to transform his regime into a workers' paradise. As Bismarck would attest, the problems of an authoritarian regime trying to woo the proletariat were not unique to France. We owe to Hendrick Nicolaas Boon, a Dutch scholar, a thorough exposition of the limitations, achievements, and failures of Napoleon III's policies in his attempt to succor the plight and to fulfill the aspirations of the new urban working classes, thereby hoping to reconcile them to the Second Empire. In the next selection, Professor David I. Kulstein gives a balanced assessment of the results of these overtures.

If the years 1848–1870 were replete with domestic political, social, and economic problems, the concurrent developments on the international scene were to present Louis-Napoleon with his greatest challenge and eventually to bring about the downfall of his regime. The outcome of the Revolutions of 1848 had resulted in a general defeat for the forces of nationalism. These forces, however, were soon to reappear—albeit in a new, hardened form. The liberals of the Frankfurt Assembly gave way to the Iron Chancellor; the idealism of Mazzini to the realism of Cavour. The German and Italian "Questions" remained in the forefront, and France literally and figuratively stood at the center of things. Napoleon III, who in any case did not need much prodding, simply could not avoid playing a leading role in the international politics of his times.

In this case the Napoleonic legend proved the severest of handicaps. The image of the first Napoleon as the son and consolidator of the Great Revolution, the champion of nationalism, may have had much appeal for the French people; but the very name of Bonaparte was enough to send shivers down the spines of the rulers of Europe whose memories of the titanic struggle of the Napoleonic era were still only too vivid. In some circles, Louis-Napoleon's election in December, 1848, may have been interpreted as a setback for the "reds"; but the advent of the Second Empire, four years later, was viewed with suspicion and alarm in more than one Foreign Office. Not without significance was Nicholas I's refusal to address him as brother.

Real or imaginary, the fear that the nephew might want to emulate his uncle seriously hindered the realization of the former's international designs. Considerations of a purely domestic order also served to complicate his task. The problem of the Papacy's temporal power, for instance, caused nagging and persistent repercussions in France. When one further keeps in mind that it is extremely difficult to conceive of a path and outcome to German and Italian unification consistent with the aims and interests of traditional French foreign policy, the complexities of the situation appear as well-nigh fathomless.

The road travelled from the reign's apogee at the Congress of Paris (1856) to the nadir of the surrender at Sedan (1870) was short and precipitous. How can this rapid decline be explained? Was Napoleon III a mad adventurer bent on duplicating his uncle's glory? Was he a well-meaning dreamer who was outwitted by the likes of Bismarck and Cavour? Was he simply ahead of his times, a farsighted ruler, who understood the need for a remapping of Europe according to the principle of self-determination for the various nationalities? Or was he a tired, sick man aimlessly drifting from one crisis to the next, and too weak to resist the pressures exerted by behind-the-scene, nefarious advisors?

This brings up the controversial question of Empress Eugénie's place in the History of the Second Empire. Many observers have argued that Napoleon III's choice of a wife was a catastrophe from all standpoints. Until the last years in exile, the imperial ménage was a classic case of incompatibility. *Cherchez la femme* is an old French dictum (practice?), and Eugénie has been assigned a large share of responsibility for the disasters that befell France in 1870–1871. Yet, was she really the evil genius of the Second Empire? We owe to Nancy Nichols Barker the most recent and scholarly study of the Empress' role in the shaping of French foreign policy. Professor Barker's verdict, at once compassionate and negative, will surely give rise to responses from Eugénie's detractors and champions alike.

In any event, the downfall of the regime brought about by France's defeat at the hands of Prussia is the one inescapable fact about the Second Empire. That is why Napoleon III's foreign policy has been and continues to be the object of severe criticism—especially on the part of French historians. Pierre Renouvin, a leading modern student of international relations, attributes the reorientation of French foreign policy to the personal intervention of the Emperor. He concludes, more in sadness than anger, that Louis-Napoleon's European policies made possible the realization of the schemes of abler men like Bismarck and Cavour. While he is somewhat more sympathetic to Napoleon III's aims, Marcel Blanchard observes that he never bothered to build up the military might which was the sine qua non of success. Siding with Prévost-Paradol, Blanchard concludes that the natural course toward the fulfillment of the *grandeur* of France was in the development of her overseas possessions. On the other hand, Albert Guérard makes a stimulating attempt to present the Emperor as the champion of the principle of nationalities, and as a firm believer in international organization. Finally, Lynn M. Case, a pioneer in the field, gives us some insights on the influence of public opinion in the formulation of foreign policy during the Second Empire. Of special interest is Professor Case's exposition of the very modern methods used by the Emperor in his attempt to ascertain the mood and aspirations of his subjects.

The third and final area of debate on the Second Empire has been waged over the nature of the regime. Here, as well, Napoleon III was confronted with severe difficulties. Not only was he faced with a problem common to all French regimes since 1789—the relentless opposition of important segments of the population, but he also had to be something of an improvisator. His power was certainly not derived from a strong hereditary claim. The mantle he inherited from the first Napoleon was hardly of the type to permit him to take his place among the "legitimate" rulers of Europe. And, as we have already mentioned, the Napoleonic legend was a dubious asset once he had actually assumed office. Nor did his power stem from well-entrenched constitutional institutions. True, the Emperor could always point to the repeated endorsement of the French nation, expressed through periodic plebiscites. Yet he never quite completely overcame the stigma of the coup d'état of December 2, 1851. An aura of illegitimacy surrounded his rule to the very end.

The analytical study of the regime is complicated by the fact that the Empire's institutions were in a constant state of flux. The authoritarianism of the early years stands in sharp contrast to the liberalism of the parliamentary revival. One thing remains quite clear, however, there was something new and modern about the whole experiment. But what did it all amount to? To Albert Guérard, the Second Empire was a pioneering experiment in "Caesarian democracy." Louis-Napoleon's merit was to have faced the implications of the dogma of absolute democracy. "The more democratic the commonwealth is, the more urgently does it need order and leadership. . . . Freedom, in the sense of *ease*, will grow in the democratic world. But liberty is something to be achieved, not the initial stage. In the terms of Louis-Napoleon himself, it must 'crown the edifice.' " Or did the dictatorship based on popular support, the denunciations of capitalism and lip service to the plight of the proletariat, and the perfection of the system of "official candidates" all presage the totalitarianism of the 20th Century? To J. Salwyn Schapiro, Louis-Napoleon was indeed a "herald" of fascism. Diametrically opposed is the opinion of Theodore Zeldin, who views the Liberal Empire as "an attempt to break the vicious circle of revolution and reaction in which France had been caught since Louis XVI." Alfred Cobban, another English scholar, concludes that the Second Empire was first and foremost "a bourgeois empire."

By way of conclusion, some overall estimates of Napoleon III and the Second Empire are presented in the last section. Pierre de La Gorce, whose monumental *Histoire du Second Empire* is a landmark in Napoleonic studies, explains why he is compelled to render a negative verdict. A. F. Thompson, whose dislike for Napoleon III, "that truly weak man," is obvious, nevertheless recognizes that "he was more than a mere plagiarist, and even careful copying might ensure a modicum of success." The selection from Marcel Blanchard's *Le Second Empire* represents a searching attempt at synthesis, on the basis of the latest scholarship. J. M. Thompson's concluding question: "Who can say past doubt that while he lived he was to be blamed, or that when he died he had failed?," can serve as a reminder that, no matter what tentative judgments we may be permitted to form on the basis of what we know about the man, the riddle of the Sphinx has yet to be solved.

René Rémond's searching comparison between the Second Empire and the Fifth Republic underlines the lingering impact of Napoleon III's reign by pointing out the continuity of a political tradition in the history of Modern France. "Bonapartism and Gaullism" is a most fitting epilogue because it lends special relevance to the study of a regime that fell a little over a century ago.

With a little effort on his part the discerning student will recognize that the body of the texts included in this book does represent a systematic and comprehensive attempt to acquaint him with the problems of the Second Empire, and to give him an appreciation of the scope and nature of the historical debate that has been, and continues to be waged over an important chapter in French history and over the man whose name appears in the heading of that chapter. Of course a problem book of this type cannot claim to be anything more than a bare introduction to the subject. The selected list of suggestions for additional readings will serve as a guide for those students whose curiosity is aroused by the selections below, and who want to probe the question further.

Conflict of Opinion

Monsieur Louis-Napoleon, you are ambitious, you aim high, but you must be told the truth. . . . You are but a rascal. Not every one who wishes to be a monster attains his wish.

VICTOR HUGO

His distinction among rulers is that he anticipated and tried to shape the future. . . . Napoleon III, the forerunner of Wilson, was in advance of French public opinion and centuries ahead of Bismarck. . . . A man may fail as Saint-Louis, Napoleon I, Lafayette, and Woodrow Wilson did fail, without being branded as a knave or a fool.

ALBERT GUÉRARD

The State has solid foundations. Bonaparte represents a class, the class of those who form a considerable majority in French society, the peasantry.

KARL MARX

The Second Empire was the real bourgeois monarchy.

ALFRED COBBAN

Can one appeal both to hereditary right and universal suffrage? Can one embark on a policy of territorial expansion and still hope to promote the self-determination of neighboring nationalities? Can one fulfill popular aspirations without sacrificing the privileges of the bourgeoisie? Can one at once monopolize political power and presume to lead the country toward greater freedom? The Second Empire was to squander its energies in an attempt to reconcile these contradictions.

ADRIEN DANSETTE

The personal concepts of Napoleon III provide us with the only real explanation for the new orientation of French foreign policy. . . . He gave the lie to [his] pacific grand designs by waging unnecessary wars in Crimea, Italy, and Mexico. . . . There was thus a flagrant contradiction between his aspirations and his deeds.

PIERRE RENOUVIN

The real significance of the Second Empire is greater today than when it flourished. The methods that it employed, the policies that it pursued, and the ideas that it proclaimed anticipated in a vague, incomplete way what is now known as "fascism."

J. SALWYN SCHAPIRO

The Liberal Empire was an attempt to break the vicious circle of revolution and reaction in which France had been caught since Louis XVI.

THEODORE ZELDIN

Who can say past doubt that while he lived he was to be blamed, or that when he died he had failed? . . . He was a man to be pitied more than to be blamed. . . . He was a man too small for the great things he set out to do.

J. M. THOMPSON

I THE MAN

Victor Hugo

NAPOLEON THE LITTLE

Victor Hugo (1802–1885), like many other great figures in French literature, played an active role in politics. Like many of his less exalted compatriots, he was a man of shifting allegiances. An ultra-royalist in his youth, he accepted a peerage from Louis-Philippe, served in the Legislative Assembly of the Second Republic, and promoted the candidacy of Louis-Napoleon in December, 1848. He was consistent, however, in his irreconcilable opposition to the Second Empire. He went into exile shortly after the coup d'état of December 2, 1851, and did not return to France until the regime had fallen. Napoléon le Petit (1852) was written in Brussels in sixteen days. The book is a sustained diatribe in which Hugo released his pent-up fury. The very title was a master stroke. The epithet "le petit" stuck, and it did widespread and lasting damage to Napoleon III's historical reputation.

Charles-Louis-Napoleon Bonaparte, born in Paris on the 20th of April, 1808, is the son of Hortense de Beauharnais, married by the Emperor to Louis Napoleon, King of Holland. In 1831, Louis Bonaparte was involved in the insurrections in Italy, where his eldest brother was killed, and tried to overthrow the Papacy. On the 30th of October, 1835, he attempted to overthrow Louis-Philippe. He failed at Strasburg, and having been pardoned by Louis-Philippe, embarked for America, leaving his accomplices behind him to be tried. On the 11th of November he wrote: "The King, *in his clemency* has ordered me to be sent to America"; he declared himself "deeply moved by the *generosity* of the King," adding: "Certainly we were all guilty of taking up arms against the Government, but I am the guiltiest of all." And he concludes thus: "I was guilty of attempting to overthrow the Government, and yet the Government has shown itself generous towards me." He returned to Switzerland from America, and was made captain of artillery at Berne and a burgher of Salenstein in Thurgau. Amid the diplomatic complications to which his presence in Switzerland gave rise, he was equally careful to avoid acknowledging a French or a Swiss nationality. To reassure the French Government, he limited himself to a declaration, in a letter of the 20th of August, 1838, that he was living "almost alone" in the house "in which his

From Victor Hugo, "Napoleon the Little," *The Works of Victor Hugo*, Vol. VIII (New York and Philadelphia: The Nottingham Society, *circa* 1907).

mother died," and that his firm intention was "to remain tranquil."
On the 6th of August, 1840, he landed at Boulogne, parodying the
landing at Cannes, with the traditional little hat on his head, bringing
a gilt eagle on top of a flag, and a live eagle in a cage, a number of
proclamations, sixty lackeys, cooks, and stableboys disguised as
French soldiers, with uniforms purchased in the Temple and buttons
of the 42nd of the line manufactured in London. He threw money to
the people walking in the streets, raised his hat on the point of his
sword, and shouted: "Vive l'Empereur;" fired a pistol at an officer,
but hit a soldier, breaking three of his teeth—and fled. He is taken,
and five hundred thousand francs in gold and banknotes are found
on him. The *procureur général* Franck-Carré says to him before the
full Court of Peers: "You attempted to corrupt soldiers by the distribution of money." The Peers condemn him to perpetual imprisonment, and he is sent to Ham. There self-communion and reflection
would seem to have ripened his mind; he wrote and published some
works which, in spite of certain ignorance of France and of the age,
were imbued with a spirit of progress and democracy. Their titles
are: "Extinction du Paupérisme," "Analyse de la Question des
Sucres," and "Idées Napoléoniennes," in which he makes the Emperor out a "humanitarian." In the "Fragments Historiques" he wrote:
"I am a citizen first, a Bonaparte after." He had already declared
himself, in 1832, a republican in his "Rêveries Politiques." After six
years' captivity, he escaped from Ham, disguised as a mason, and
took refuge in England. When February came, he hailed the Republic, took his seat as Representative of the People in the Constituent
Assembly, mounted the tribune on the 21st of September, 1848, and
said: "All my life will be devoted to the consolidation of the Republic," published a manifesto which may be summarized in two lines:
liberty, progress, democracy, amnesty, abolition of decrees of proscription and of banishment; was elected President by five million
five hundred thousand votes, swore fealty solemnly to the Constitution of the 20th of December, 1848, and destroyed it on the 2nd of
December, 1851. In the interval he had crushed the Roman Republic,
and restored in 1849 that Papacy which in 1831 he had attempted to
overthrow; he had, moreover, taken some part or other in the shady
transaction called the "Lottery of the ingots of gold." In the weeks
preceding the coup d'état, this money-bag had become transparent,
and a hand was perceived in it resembling his. On the 2nd of

December and the following days, he, the Executive Power, assailed the Legislative Power, arrested the Representatives, drove away the Assembly, dissolved the Council of State, expelled the High Court of Justice, suppressed the laws, took twenty-five millions from the Bank, gorged the army with gold, mowed down Paris with grape-shot, and struck terror into France. Since then, he has proscribed eighty-four Representatives of the People, robbed the Princes of Orleans of the property of their father, to whom he owed his life, decreed despotism in fifty-eight articles under the title of a constitution, garotted the Republic, turned the sword of France into a gag in the mouth of liberty, jobbed in railway shares, rifled the pockets of the people, regulated the budget by a ukase, deported ten thousand democrats to Africa and Cayenne, exiled forty thousand republicans to Belgium, Spain, Piedmont, Switzerland, and England, and brought anguish to every soul and a blush to every brow.

Louis Bonaparte thinks he is ascending a throne; he does not perceive that he is climbing a gibbet.

Louis Bonaparte is a man of middle height, cold, pale, and heavy. He has the look of a person who is not quite awake. He has published, as we have already related, a work of some value on artillery, and has a thorough acquaintance with the management of cannon. He rides well. There is a slight German drawl in his words. As to his histrionic abilities, he gave an exhibition of them in the Eglinton tournament. He wears a thick mustache, hiding a smile like the duke of Alba's, and has the lackluster eye of Charles IX.

Judged outside of what he calls "his necessary acts" or "his great acts," he is a vulgar fellow, childish, theatrical, and vain. The persons invited by him to Saint-Cloud in summer, receive with the invitation an order to bring an evening and morning dress. He is fond of tufts, trimmings, spangles, top-knots, and embroideries, of grand words and grand titles, of sound and glitter and all the petty glories and glass beads of power. His kinship to the battle of Austerlitz entitles him to dress as a general. He does so.

This man would stain the second plane of history; he defiles the first. To be despised affects him little: the appearance of respect contents him. Europe, pointing to Haiti, was laughing at the other continent when she saw this white Souloque make his appearance. There is now in Europe, deep sunk in every mind, even beyond the limits of France, a feeling of profound stupefaction, a feeling of

FIGURE 2. The epithet "le petit" long remained attached to Napoleon III's name. This bitter caricature accuses the Emperor of treason during the Franco-Prussian War, calls for his being condemned to penal servitude, and invites all "honest citizens" to spit in his face. (*Photo. Bibl. nat. Paris*)

something like a personal indignity; for the interests of Europe, whether she wills or not, are incorporated with those of France, and whatever degrades the one humiliates the other.

Before the 2nd of December, it was a common saying among the leaders of the Right with regard to Louis Bonaparte: "He is an idiot." They were mistaken. Certainly that brain of his is muddy, has gaps here and there; but thoughts logically connected and interlinked may, to some extent, be discerned in places. It is a book from which certain pages have been torn out. Louis Bonaparte is a man of one fixed idea, but a fixed idea is not idiocy. He knows what he wants, and marches to his aim. Over justice, over law, over reason, honour, and humanity, if you will, he still marches to his aim.

He is not an idiot. He is a man of other times than ours. He seems absurd and mad because he has no counterpart. Transport him to Spain in the sixteenth century, and Philip II will recognize him; to England, and Henry VIII will smile on him; to Italy, and Caesar Borgia will throw his arms about his neck. Or even confine yourself to placing him outside of European civilization; drop him at Yanina in 1817, Ali Tepelini will tender him his hand.

There are elements of the Middle Ages and the Lower Empire in him. His deeds would seem quite natural to Michael Ducas, to Romanes Diogenes, to Nicephorus Botoniates, to the eunuch Narses, to the vandal Stilicho, to Mahomet II, to Alexander VI, to Ezzelino of Padua, and they seem quite natural to him; only, he forgets or is ignorant that in the times in which we live his actions have to traverse those great currents of human morality loosened by our three centuries of learning and enlightenment and by the French Revolution, and that in the society he belongs to his actions will assume their true form and show forth in all their native hideousness.

His partisans—he has some—are ready to draw a parallel between his uncle, the first Bonaparte, and him. They say: "One made the 18th of Brumaire, the other has made the 2nd of December, one was eager for power, so is the other." The first Bonaparte wished to restore the Empire of the West, to make Europe his vassal, to dominate the continent by his power and dazzle it by his greatness, to sit on a chair of state and give footstools to kings, to make history say, "Nimrod, Cyrus, Alexander, Hannibal, Caesar, Charlemagne, Napoleon," to be a master of the world. And he was. For this he made the 18th of Brumaire. The second Bonaparte wishes to have horses and mistresses, to be called Monseigneur, and to live well. For this he has made the 2nd of December. Eager for power both. Yes, the comparison is just. Let us add that, like the first, he too would be emperor. But what renders the comparison a little more tranquillizing is the circumstance that there is perhaps some difference between conquering the empire and filching it.

Be that as it may, one fact is certain, and cannot be concealed even by the dazzling curtain of glory and misfortune on which are

written, Arcola, Lodi, the Pyramids, Eylau, Friedland, St. Helena—
one fact, we repeat, is certain, and it is that the 18th of Brumaire is
a crime, the stain of which on the memory of Napoleon has been
magnified by the 2nd of December. . . .

Be tranquil! History has him in its grip. Still, if to be laid hold of by
history flatters the vanity of Monsieur Bonaparte; if he chance to have
(and really it looks like it) any mental illusion as to his value as a
political scoundrel—let him discard it. He must not imagine that
because he has piled horror on horror he will ever be able to hoist
himself up to the level of the great bandits of history. We have done
wrong, perhaps, in some pages of this work to draw a parallel
between him and these men. No; although he has committed great
crimes, he himself remains paltry. He will never be anything but the
nocturnal strangler of liberty; he will never be anything but the man
who intoxicated soldiers—not with glory, as did the first Napoleon,
but with wine; he will never be anything but the pygmy tyrant of a
great people. The stature of the individual is entirely incompatible
with greatness, even in infamy. As a dictator, he is a buffoon; as
emperor, he will be grotesque. That will finish him. It will be his destiny
to make the human race shrug its shoulders. Will his punishment be
the less harsh on account of this? No; disdain in no way lessens
resentment. He will be hideous, and he will continue ridiculous—
nothing more. History, while laughing at him, smites him. Even the
indignation of the most indignant cannot get him out of this position.
Great thinkers take a delight in chastising great despots, and sometimes enlarge them a little to render them worthy of their wrath; but
what can the historian do with such a personage as this? The historian can only lead him to posterity by the ear. The man once
stripped of his success, the pedestal taken away, the tinsel and the
glitter and the big sword removed, the poor little skeleton left naked
and shivering—can anything be imagined more beggarly and pitiful?

History has its tigers. Historians, the immortal guardians of fero-
cious animals, exhibit this imperial menagerie to the nations. Tacitus
alone, that great belluarius, has caught and imprisoned eight or ten
of those tigers in the iron cages of his style. Gaze on them! They
are terrific and superb; their spots form a part of their beauty. Look,
yonder is Nimrod, the hunter of men; this is Busiris, the tyrant of
Egypt; this is Phalaris, who roasted men in his brazen bull, in order
to make the bull bellow; this is Ahasuerus, who tore the skin from

the heads of the seven Maccabees and then had them roasted alive; this is Nero, who burned Rome and covered the Christians with wax and pitch and lit them as torches; this is Tiberius, the man of Capri; this is Domitian; this is Caracalla; this is Heliogabalus; that other is Commodus, who to his other horrible merits has added that of being the son of Marcus Aurelius; those are the czars, those others the sultans; those are the popes (among them notice the tiger Borgia); yonder is Philip called the Good, as the furies were called Eumenides; yonder is Richard III, sinister and deformed; that is Henry VIII, with his huge belly and broad face, who killed two of his five wives and ripped up one; this is Christian II, the Nero of the North; that is Philip II, the demon of the South. They are appalling; harken to their roars, observe them one after another. The historian leads them before you; he drags them to the edge of their cage, opens their mighty jaws, shows you their teeth, and their claws. You may say of each, "That is a royal tiger." In fact, they have been caught on all the thrones of earth. History conducts them through the ages; she will not let them die; she takes care of them. They are her tigers; she does not mix them with the jackals; she puts and keeps apart the filthy beasts.

Monsieur Bonaparte will be, with Claudius, with Ferdinand VII of Spain, with Ferdinand II of Naples, in the cage of the hyenas. There is a little of the brigand about him, but much more of the trickster. He always gives you the impression of the poor blackleg-prince who lived by his wits in England; his present prosperity, his triumph, his empire, and his self-importance, do not affect you in the least; the purple mantle trails over boots down at the heels. Napoleon the Little —nothing more, nothing less; the title of this book is a good one. The meanness of his vices is injurious to the greatness of his crimes. Just consider. Pedro the Cruel massacred but did not steal; Henry III assassinated but did not swindle; Timur crushed children under the feet of his horses, pretty much as Monsieur Bonaparte has exterminated women and old men on the boulevard, but he did not lie. Listen to the Arabian historian:

Timur-Beg, Sahekeran (master of the world and of the century, master of the planetary conjunctions), was born at Kesch in 1336; he butchered one hundred thousand captives. When he was besieging Siwas, the inhabitants, to move him, sent a thousand little children bearing each a Koran on its head, and crying, "Allah! Allah!" He had the sacred books *removed with respect, and the children crushed under the hoofs of his horses. He used seventy thousand heads, together with cement, stone, and brick, in building towers at Herat, Sebzvar, Tekrit, Aleppo, and Bagdad. He detested falsehood; when he pledged his word, he could be trusted.*

Monsieur Bonaparte does not reach this stature. He is without the dignity which the great despots of the East and West blend with their ferocity. He lacks the majestic proportions of the Caesars. To be the counterpart and semblance of all those executioners who have tortured humanity for four thousand years, a man must not be a cross between a general of division and a mountebank on the Champs Elysées; he must not have been a policeman at London; he must not have wiped from his face, with eyes cast down, in the open Court of Peers, the scornful insults of M. Magnan; he must not have been called pickpocket by the English journals; he must not have been menaced with Clichy; he must not, in a word, be a scamp.

Monsieur Louis-Napoleon, you are ambitious, you aim high, but you must be told the truth. Now, what do you wish we should do in this matter? It is all very well for you to realize, by overthrowing the tribune, the wish of Caligula after your own fashion, "Would that the human race had but a single head, that I might cut it off at one stroke"; it is all very well for you to banish republicans by thousands, as Philip III expelled the Moors, and as Torquemada hunted the Jews, it is all very well for you to have casemates like Pedro the Cruel, prison-ships like Hariadan, dragonnades like Père Letellier, and dungeons like Ezzelino III, to be a perjurer like Ludovico Sforza, a murderer and assassin of his subjects like Charles IX—it is all very well for you to act in this manner: you do so in vain. When we hear your name, you can never make us connect it with theirs in our minds; you are but a rascal. Not every one who wishes to be a monster attains his wish.

G. P. Gooch

THE EMPEROR

George Peabody Gooch (1873–1968), an Honorary Fellow of Trinity College, Cambridge University, was eighty-seven years old when The Second Empire *was published in 1960. The liveliness of his approach, to what was for him a relatively new subject, might well be the envy of a man half his age. Gooch's reputation as a scholar, his many interests and activities, and the number and quality of his publications on a broad variety of topics, all served to make him one of the grand old men of the historical profession. The selection below bears Gooch's trademark as an indefatigable culler of letters, memoirs, and diaries. Over and beyond the author's own estimate, which is expressed in unmistakable terms, the reader is presented with a portrait of Napoleon III as depicted by a number of his contemporaries.*

Napoleon the Little, as Victor Hugo called him, was a pocket edition of his mighty uncle, but a far better man. Josephine called her grandson *Oui Oui* because he was so good-tempered; Bismarck thought his intellect overrated, his heart underrated. The greatest of soldiers was the super-egoist of all time—"as great as a man can be without virtue" in Tocqueville's incisive phrase . . . France was his instrument, not his fatherland. "If you would rule mankind," he declared, "the heart must break or turn to stone." For him the choice was easy. The heart of Louis-Napoleon never turned to stone. "I love and respect him," declared Conneau, the faithful doctor who stood at his side from youth to old age and knew all his failings. "He loved the people," declares La Gorce, the fairest of his judges, "not particularly his own, but all peoples, that is to say the poor, the weak, the disinherited." Could that have been said of any previous ruler of France, even of Henry IV? There was a benevolence, occasionally an almost feminine gentleness, in him which we miss in the executioner of the Duc d'Enghien. His greatest qualities, testifies Véron, the influential Editor of *Le Constitutionnel,* were gratitude and generosity. The Fourth Estate was knocking at the door, and he earnestly sought to improve its lot. "La guerre," exclaimed the fallen Emperor to the youthful Lord John Russell on a visit to Elba, "c'est un bon jeu, une belle occupation." "I hope some day to command a great army,"

From G. P. Gooch, *The Second Empire* (London, 1960). Reprinted by permission of Longmans, Green, & Co., Limited.

confided the prisoner at Ham to his former playmate Hortense Cornu. "I know I should distinguish myself. I feel I possess every military quality." Yet, when at Solferino he saw what war was like, his heart bled at the butchery. When all is said for the most humane and the most likeable of dictators, it would have been better for France and the world had he never been born. Uncle and nephew alike were gamblers who plunged their country into avoidable conflicts and had to learn at the expense of France that, in Byron's words, "tempted fate would leave the loftiest star." That they died in exile unmourned by their former subjects tells its own sorry tale.

When Napoleon divorced Josephine, he remained on excellent terms with her family, and liked to have Hortense and her boys play about the Court. Her youngest son retained dim memories of the man whose words and deeds filled his mind and fashioned his career. On the eve of the Emperor's departure for his last battle the boy knelt before him and burst into tears. "My governess says that you are going to the wars," he cried. *"Ne partez pas, ne partez pas."* The Emperor, deeply moved, embraced him, saying to someone in attendance: "He will have a good heart. Perhaps he is the hope of my race." When the curtain fell at St. Helena in 1821 the boy of thirteen wrote to his mother: "In Paris I was so young that it is only in my heart that I have any memory of him. When I do wrong, if I think of this great man I seem to feel his spirit within me bidding me be worthy of his name." To his aged grandmother he wrote: "You can imagine how welcome is the blessing of the mother of the Emperor, for I venerate him as a god." They were all pygmies compared with him, he exclaimed, but even a pygmy might carry on a giant's work.

Born in 1808, Louis-Napoleon scarcely knew his morose father who, after a brief span on the throne of Holland, retired to sulk in Florence, leaving his younger son with Hortense. On the fall of the Empire the Duchess of Saint-Leu, as she was called, made her home at Arenenberg at the northern end of Lake Constance, where she devoted herself to music, painting, and society. Though she dearly loved her son, she and his first governor, Abbé Bertrand, did nothing to train his mind. A wiser choice was made when the lad was twelve, for Philippe le Bas, son of Robespierre's comrade in the National Convention, brought a rare combination of qualities to his task—tact, patience, enthusiasm, wide culture, a deep sense of responsibility, and a loving heart. For the next eight years master and pupil were inseparable, at home, on travel, and during his schooldays at Augsburg. His difficulties and triumphs are recorded in the tutor's correspondence with his family published in 1903. From the first he was amazed by the contrast between the warmth of his pupil's heart and the almost unbelievable inertia of his brain. "I am very satisfied with my pupil," he wrote after six weeks. "Docility and an excellent heart would make a personality of distinction if they were accompanied by industry and quicker apprehension. At twelve he is like a boy of seven, unfamiliar with even the simplest things, and finding it extremely difficult to express even what he does understand. I don't think it is a lack of intelligence, but rather an inactive and inattentive mind. With patience it will improve, but it will not be easy. I already notice some progress and so does the dear child. The difficulty will be to make him love his lessons." At the close of the year 1820 he reported a further advance. "The obstacle would have baffled anyone with less courage than myself. An excellent heart, sweet-tempered, but a horror of work and a desolating ignorance." Now there were signs of interest in history and literature, and he had begun to read with enjoyment. Twelve months later he had become a model pupil. The tutor's first impression was correct: there was plenty of intelligence. What had been lacking was the complete incapacity of his former tutor to make lessons interesting. When master and pupil parted in 1828, the latter was interested in many things and ready to play his part in the world.

His faith in his star was sustained by a series of occurrences which gave him his chance. His elder brother had died in childhood, the next was struck down by fever during the Carbonari rising in 1831, and in the following year his cousin, the Duc de Reichstadt, faded away at Schönbrunn. When *l'Aiglon* was gone, he became the recognized standard-bearer of the Bonaparte cause. Meeting him for the first time in his mother's house in Rome in 1829, Lord Malmesbury described him as "a wild, harum-scarum youth, riding at full gallop down the streets to the peril of the public, fencing and pistol-shooting, and apparently without serious thoughts of any kind, though even then he was possessed with the conviction that he would some day rule over France. His face was grave and dark, but redeemed by a singularly bright smile." Of the superman's brothers, Joseph had no son, Lucien had ceased to count after Brumaire, and Louis was a sour misanthrope without a friend. The road was open. Realizing that

France had had enough of war, he turned his thoughts to the problems of peace. His ideal of government was an efficient and paternal autocracy resting on nationwide assent. The great Emperor had promised constitutional reform in the *Acte Additionel* during the Hundred Days, though whether his pledge would have materialized had the verdict of Waterloo gone the other way we may doubt. His nephew coquetted with a similar notion, and the promise of a Liberal Empire was implemented in a rather half-hearted way at the close of his reign. While the *Petit Caporal* had regarded the masses primarily as cannon-fodder, his successor thought of them as subordinate partners in a national task. Inheriting the conception of paternalism from the Enlightened Despots of the eighteenth century, he aspired, not wholly without success, to deserve the proud title assigned to himself by Frederick the Great: *le premier domestique de l'état* . . . .

Only the few who knew him well, like his mother and Persigny, took the young dreamer seriously. After a visit to Arenenberg, Talleyrand's niece, the Duchesse de Dino, reported that he was "no greater danger to the July Monarchy than a student at the École Polytechnique, a good mathematician, a good horseman, but timid and silent like a well brought up girl."

Convinced that he alone was able to give France what she needed, the Pretender raised his standard in a *putsch* at Strassbourg in 1836. After the bloodless fiasco which lasted two hours he received the mild sentence of banishment to the United States. "A deplorable acquittal," commented Metternich, obsessed by memories of the First Empire. "What lies ahead? Disorder followed by the despotism of the masses or of individuals." Returning to Europe in the following year to close his mother's eyes, he settled in London where he studied the working of Constitutional Monarchy and composed the longest and most important of his political tracts, *Les idées napoléoniennes,* published in 1839. Utilizing the narratives of the Napoleonic era which were pouring from the press, he piled incense on the hero's altar . . . .

Louis-Napoleon was no orator, but he knew how to handle a pen. "If the Emperor cares for my verdict," declared Beranger, "tell him that I regard him as the first writer of the century." While dictators usually start from scratch, he sailed into fame under his uncle's flag. The Napoleonic saga was taking shape. *Parle-nous de lui, grand-mère, Parle-nous de lui,* chanted Béranger. In the words of

Victor Hugo, his candidature dated from Austerlitz. To bring back his bones was a good beginning, but why not bring back his throne? He had learned every detail of the twilight years at St. Helena direct from Gourgaud and Montholon; the demigod obsessed him. It was almost a case of dual personality. *Toujours Lui, Lui partout.* His picture was found in the peasant's cottage beside that of Christ and the Virgin Mother.

The five and a half years in the fortress of Ham, though alleviated by study, authorship, and visitors, might well have broken an ordinary mortal, but the Prince's belief in his destiny was unimpaired. General Montholon, who had shared the Emperor's exile at St. Helena, Conneau, the family doctor, a valet, and a village girl who bore him two sons, were a consolation. Hortense Cornu, daughter of his mother's former lady-in-waiting, procured him books and looked up references, and he dabbled in chemical experiments. Literature, except for Schiller's stirring dramas, gave him little pleasure. When in later years people expressed surprise at the extent of his knowledge, he answered with a smile: "Do you forget my years of study at the university of Ham?" He was never a man to be idle, and he knew how to wait. "I have no wish to be elsewhere," he wrote during the first winter. "Here is my right place. With my name I must be either in the gloom of a dungeon or in the glare of power." "I have faith," he wrote to a friend in 1842, "the faith which makes men endure all things with resignation and makes them trample underfoot all joys, the faith which alone can move mountains." "If I have miraculously escaped every danger," he added three years later, "if my soul is steadfast in face of so many disappointments, it is because I have a mission." To his cousin, Prince Napoleon, he wrote:

> I pass my time in studying, reflecting and hoping. I regret nothing I have done. I am sure the shade of the Emperor protects and blesses me. I am not unhappy, for I do not feel that my sufferings are in vain. I am convinced that I have done my duty—the only member of the family to do so —for I have sacrificed my youth, my fortune, my life to the triumph of the cause which we cannot desert without dishonour.

The tribute to himself was deserved, for no other member of the clan lifted a finger to revive its fortunes. When offered release in return for renunciation of his claims and a promise to abstain from

NAPOLÉON LOUIS DANS SA CAPTIVITÉ A HAM

further attempts to overthrow the regime, the pariah of Europe, as he described himself, declined. In addition to contributing to the provincial press, he published booklets on the extinction of pauperism and unemployment by agricultural colonies, on the sugar beet industry, on artillery, and on the desirability of a Nicaraguan canal.

"I found him little changed," reported Lord Malmesbury in April, 1845. "He confessed that though his confidence and courage were unabated he was weary of his prison, from which he saw no chance of escaping, as he knew that the French Government gave him opportunities of doing so that they might shoot him in the act." "My power is in an immortal name and in that only; but I have waited long enough, and I cannot endure imprisonment any longer." His visitor returned to London deeply impressed with his calm resolution. "Very few in a miserable prison like this, isolated and quasi-forgotten, would have kept their intellect braced by constant studies and original compositions." A year later, when repairs were needed in his rooms, he disguised himself in the clothes of a workman brought in by his valet, carried a plank on his shoulder, walked quietly out, and entered Belgium with a British passport supplied by a friend. Turning up unexpectedly in London, he was welcomed by old friends, among them Disraeli and other members of Lady Blessington's lively circle in Kensington, and served as a Special Constable when the Chartist demonstrations in 1848 alarmed the capital. "Evidently a weak fellow," commented Cobden, "but mild and amiable." Still waters run deep. . . .

A vivid portrait of the Prince is painted in the correspondence of Lord Cowley, who arrived in Paris as British Ambassador a few weeks after the coup. "To fathom his thoughts or divine his intentions would try the powers of the most clear-sighted. No one's advice seems to affect him. He seems a strange mixture of good and evil. Few approach him who are not charmed by his manners. I am told that an angry word never escapes him. His determination of purpose needs no comment." The portrait by Hübner, the Austrian Ambassador, is much the same. "What a singular man! What a mixture of

FIGURE 3. Louis-Napoleon devoted long hours to studying and writing during the six years (1840–1846) he spent in prison at the "University" of Ham. He also enjoyed the favors of a comely country lass who bore him two sons. (*Photo. Bibl. nat. Paris*)

opposites! Calculating and naive, pleasure-loving and fond of marvels, sometimes sincere, sometimes impenetrable, ever a conspirator. . . ."

At the close of the first decade of dictatorship clouds began to gather. All pretense of affection between husband and wife had disappeared; Prince Napoleon was a thorn in the flesh, and Princess Mathilde was rarely seen at Court. The death of Morny in 1865 was regarded by the British ambassador as a great loss. Dictators are lonely men, and of his Ministers Persigny alone could be described as a friend. . . . [The latter], who understood and loved his master, almost broke his heart over the rapid decline, which he attributed to a congenital lack of toughness. Without the extreme kindliness which distinguished him, he writes in his Memoirs, a gentleness so attractive in a private citizen but so dangerous in a prince, he would not have had such Ministers or at any rate would not have let them abuse his consideration.

So it all comes back to his character. It is impossible not to love and respect him, but he lacked a quality essential to great princes—severity, the faculty to punish as well as to reward. To see him at close quarters, as simple and modest in his brilliant fortune as the least of his subjects, the perfect gentleman without a shadow of personal pride or vanity, applying to every topic the greatest good sense, the most intrepid of men in moments of peril, it is impossible not to be charmed and conquered, and one understands the grandeurs of his reign. But if one looks deeper into his nature and witnesses the strife between his reason and his kindly heart, one pities this prince, so generous, so indulgent, for being unable to punish those who deserve punishment. How easily can this noble spirit be the victim of intrigue! Hence his errors, weakness, and frustrations at home and abroad. With such a prince surrounded by men of sincerity and conviction dedicated to a great cause, what lofty achievements would be possible we can judge by the beginning of the reign before intriguers discovered how far they could go with him and abuse his trust. So kindly a prince ceased to be feared, and selfish intriguers were assured of their victory in advance. He once said to me: Ah! Persigny, what a pity you are so angry! What a pity you are not! I replied. If you, like me, could not suppress your indignation against evil, injustice, and intrigue, everyone would do his duty, which no one does now. Remember the wrath of Achilles. Why did not God give you this generous wrath which terrifies evildoers and rewards the good?

. . . When Lord Lyons, an experienced observer, succeeded Lord Cowley in the British Embassy at the end of 1867 he pronounced that the Empire was in decline. "The discontent is great and the distress among the working classes severe. There is no glitter at home or abroad to divert public attention, and the French have spent a good many years without the excitement of a change." In the summer of 1868 he described the Emperor as much out of spirits, since, though the country districts were still on his side, all the towns were against him. "Probably the wisest thing he could do would be to allow real Parliamentary government so as to give the Opposition hope of coming into office by less violent means than a revolution." A year later he wrote: "I have an instinct that they will drift into a republic before the year is over." In the elections of May 1869, the votes for the Government were only in the proportion of four to three; the large cities, at no time very friendly, were growing rapidly hostile. Historians emphasize the ruler's waning health as a major factor in the decline and fall. The Liberal Empire with Ollivier as its standard-bearer was disapproved by the Empress, Rouher, Persigny, and other authoritarians as a tacit admission that he had lost faith in himself. In 1866 Metternich reported that he could neither walk nor sleep nor hardly eat, and by 1870 he was always in pain. He had never rationed his dissipations, and the torturing stone in the bladder weakened his grip. The last time Mme Octave Feuillet saw him was at a reception at the house of Princess Mathilde shortly before the crisis of 1870. "He sat sombre and silent. His wan, expressionless eyes were fixed on the oriental carpet at his feet. The Empress appeared equally sombre. On the way out, he whispered to her: Quick. I am in horrible pain."

. . . The regime which had opened with a fanfare and had dazzled Europe for almost twenty years fell with a crash. The shattered Regent, in danger of her life, fled to Deauville in the carriage of the American dentist, Dr. Evans, and crossed the Channel, while General Trochu and Gambetta took over national defense. The crowning disaster was the surrender of Bazaine with his large army in beleaguered Metz, after which Paris was slowly starved and bombarded into surrender. The war was over, but not the suffering of the capital. The Paris Commune seized control, burned the Tuileries, and was in turn mercilessly suppressed by the government of Thiers. For two more years the fallen autocrat, now a mere shadow of his old self, lived quietly with his family at Chislehurst, visited by Queen Victoria and other old friends, watching with loving pride the growth to manhood of his devoted son, occasionally seeking a change at Torquay, Brighton, or Cowes. "I always found him simple and good, charitable and full of kindness," declared Eugénie, now fully reconciled to her wayward partner. "He endured contradiction and calumny with admirable equanimity, and when disaster overwhelmed us he carried his stoicism and meekness to the point of sublimity. If you could have seen him during his last years at Chislehurst! Never a word of complaint or recrimination!" Lord Malmesbury found him much more depressed by the sufferings of France than by his own misfortunes. "His quiet and calm dignity and absence of all nerviness and irritability, were the grandest examples of moral courage than the severest stoic could have imagined. I confess I was never more moved." . . . Queen Victoria rightly pronounced him "a very extraordinary man." Such people—half idealists, half adventurers—rarely make satisfactory rulers, and dictators usually end by destroying themselves through military ambition or blind folly. In the words of Hübner, the Austrian Ambassador, he had only one principle and that a superstition—a belief in his star.

Adrien Dansette

LOUIS-NAPOLEON: A VIGNETTE

A graduate of the Ecole des Sciences Politiques and a Doctor of Law, Adrien Dansette (b. 1901) is at once Vice President of an insurance company and one of the most prolific students of modern French history. He is thus one of the very few people who have managed to combine business with scholarship. Dansette, who is best known for his many studies on the Third Republic, is now at work on a projected six-volume Histoire du Second Empire. This selection is taken from the conclusion of the first volume of what promises to be an important contribution to Napoleonic studies. The author's searching questions, delineating the inherent contradictions of Napoleon III and his regime, are especially noteworthy.

The new Sovereign—in fact, if still without the official title—was not lacking either in intelligence or character. The passing years have led to a better appreciation of a mind that grasped the growing importance of socio-economic problems, anticipated the formation of a European Community, understood the need for the reorganization of the French Army, and devised a system of government which, by enlisting nationalism and socialism in the service of personal power, foreshadowed certain authoritarian regimes of the Twentieth Century. Louis-Napoleon's sense of the future places him above average among the pretenders and politicians of his day. This faculty, essential in anyone who would lay claim to statesmanship, can be quite dangerous when it is mixed, as it was in his case, with a predilection for premature dreams and a certain neglect of immediate realities.

Far from setting him apart, these defects were those of many of his contemporaries. Louis-Napoleon was truly a man of his times; and, after all, he lived in the Romantic era. Had he not been born a Bonaparte, he would certainly have become one of those men of 1848, whose generous outlook and humanitarian aspirations he shared, and whom he was to persecute against his innermost wishes. But, and that is the key to an understanding of the man, this outlook and these aspirations had to be blended with the Napoleonic heri-

From Adrien Dansette, *Louis-Napoléon à la conquête du pouvoir (Histoire du Second Empire,* Vol. I) (Paris, 1961). Reprinted by permission of Librairie Hachette. Editor's translation.

tage. That is why his ideology was somewhat disparate. The most important of his concepts had been formulated before he reached the age of twenty-five. Equally alien to the royalist legitimism of the Restoration, the bourgeois liberalism of the July Monarchy, and the republican individualism of the French Revolution, he disliked the old nobility which he dismissed as decadent, and he showed little interest in a bourgeoisie whose qualities and defects he was in no position to measure. But, having been exposed to the way of life of the common man in Switzerland, he was strongly attracted by the people. In his testament Napoleon III was to echo Napoleon I's motto: *"Everything for the French people."*[1] It was his belief that the nation, expressing its will through universal suffrage, should confer power on the heir of the chosen dynasty. Freed from the sterile and ineffective squabbling of parliamentarism, and backed by the Army, this power could effectively promote the *grandeur* of France: at home, by stimulating the economy through great works sponsored by the State and large corporations; abroad, by the revision of the Treaties of 1815, and the fulfillment of the national aspirations of subject peoples.

Louis-Napoleon's character was equally arresting. As docteur Véron once said: *"France is always on the side of those Princes who show contempt for money and death."*[2] The hero of Saint-Helena had left both a memorial and a progeny. The nephew believed in the truth of the "Memorial," and in his own destiny as the leader of a chosen House. He has sometimes been labelled a "visionary." Events were to show that his vision was no mirage. As early as 1830, when the Duke of Reichstadt and Napoleon-Louis still outranked him in the dynastic order, he unhesitatingly risked his life and freedom. He remained of a piece after he became the Emperor's heir, and he never wavered in the faith that his cause would win out sooner or later. Nor did he ever fail to identify his cause with that of France. For twenty years he fought on relentlessly, almost alone, in spite of his family, through thick and thin, always rising above the bitterness of defeat. He triumphed in the end, as he had always known he would, because he was "a born, imperturbable, and farseeing conspirator."

[1] Dansette's italics—Ed.
[2] Dansette's italics—Ed.

He has been caricatured by his enemies, and praised indiscriminately by his friends. Few statesmen have been at once less understood and so difficult to understand. The originality of a "complex" and "strong" personality (to use Renan's words) escapes summary judgments based on its most salient characteristics. Further scrutiny reveals that these same characteristics were rounded or counterbalanced by less obvious traits. His impassive composure hid an emotional and sensitive nature, and his habitual taciturnity sometimes gave way to touching effusions. A kindhearted man capable of the most delicate gestures, he was careless in the selection of his paramours. An instinctive aristocrat, he surrounded himself with adventurers. He was at once sceptical of human nature and faithful in the extreme to his friends; sincere, loyal, and deceitful to the point of treachery; apathetic and given to long periods of sustained activity; magnanimous and ruthless in the fulfilling of "his mission." He was highly receptive to new ideas so long as they were compatible with his own, but retreated into dogmatism whenever the least tenet of his doctrine was challenged. If his solitary meditations had taught him to take the long range point of view, he was anything but perspicacious when it came to the evaluation of immediate possibilities. Seemingly without an answer to objections and puzzled by problems, thus appearing to equivocate, he would suddenly announce irreversible decisions which he had long since arrived at in secret. These, then, were some of the contradictions in the enigmatic personality of Louis-Napoleon. As Napoleon III he was later to display others.

It remains to be seen how the years were to transform the resolute conqueror of power into a wavering, fumbling emperor. It remains to be seen, and that is but another facet of the same question, how the master of France put his heterogeneous political philosophy into practice. Can one appeal both to hereditary right and universal suffrage? Can one embark on a policy of territorial expansion and still hope to promote the self-determination of neighboring nationalities? Can one fulfill popular aspirations without sacrificing the privileges of the bourgeoisie? Can one at once monopolize political power and presume to lead the country toward greater freedom? The Second Empire was to squander its energies in an attempt to reconcile these contradictions.

Roger L. Williams

THE MORTAL NAPOLEON III

Educated at Colorado College (A.B. 1947) and the University of Michigan (M.A. 1948; Ph.D. 1951), Roger L. Williams (b. 1923) is Professor and Chairman of the History Department at the University of Wyoming. The wide range of topics covered in his numerous publications attests to his versatility. He is best known, however, for his penetrating and imaginative works on the Second Empire. The conclusions reached by Professor Williams in The Mortal Napoleon III *are based on a thorough scrutiny of the Emperor's medical record. This is a type of evidence which historians have long overlooked.*

As Erik H. Erikson has pointed out, Freud's most important contribution to modern medicine lay not in those formulas about personality development that we call Freudian, but in a "technique of observation." If we are really to understand or to appreciate the men who have affected history, we must endeavor to observe them as complete individuals. To that task we have to bring, beyond the historian's ability to evaluate sources, the resolve to be open-minded and objective. As our ability to see others depends in no small way upon both our readiness and ability to see ourselves honestly, this particular genre of history seems fraught with special peril. That we can never know the absolute truth about another individual, living or dead, constitutes a lesser hazard in embarking upon such research, because we are forced to recognize at the outset that we are engaged in an essay in probability.

We historians have not been alone in our traditional reluctance to accept medical evidence. Physicians, too, know how easy it can be to exaggerate the influence of disease upon an individual; one of them, who has otherwise been generously helpful to me in my study, has written that "medical men [should] be ready to protest at being jockeyed into a false position by superficial historians." It is only fair to record, therefore, that this particular physician thought that Napoleon III's case was interesting, but that it did not involve "any startling or dramatic features and certainly . . . no disclosures of a psychiatric character so attractive nowadays to the lay writer." The

From Roger L. Williams, *The Mortal Napoleon III* (copyright © 1971 by Princeton University Press): pp. 5–7, 88–90, 191–193. Reprinted by permission of Princeton University Press. Footnotes omitted.

validity of my dissent will, of course, be judged by each reader, as I propose to show that the most significant of the emperor's ailments was a neurosis that he overcame. But the neurosis reveals to us the origin of a major problem that in fact did affect the history of the Second Empire.

Even on a more general level, historians have been somewhat neglectful of the influence of disease upon the history of mankind. Although we readily accept as factual the devastating impact of a plague upon a society, we have been slower to recognize that, since many of the diseases from which we suffer as individuals are unknown in the state of nature, history and disease are in fact inseparable. To a significant degree this unhappy equation came about because evolution did not prepare our diencephalon (that part of the brain-stem that regulates bodily activity) for that artificial environment we call civilization. Some of these diseases, gout for example, merit the historian's special interest because of a notable predilection for people of power and wealth, so that they are in the forefront of those diseases that have influenced the history of civilization. . . .

Napoleon III had available to him, in sum, the best that French medicine could supply, but that in itself could not guarantee that he would in fact receive the caliber of care that was so immediately available. In the twentieth century we take it for granted that people of high political or social rank command and obtain the best that medicine can provide and that when the doctor prescribes the patient obeys, no matter how powerful he may be. The attitude of patients and doctors, especially surgeons, a hundred years ago was very different. Before the democratization of Western society and the remarkable advances in medical science, which combined to produce the attitudes we know today, surgeons were timid when forced to prescribe for people of high rank. The elder Baron Corvisart had always advised Napoleon I, when ill, to go to a military hospital, where he would be treated the same as any lieutenant or captain would be, rather than to be treated at the Tuileries where the fear of responsibility paralyzed the intelligence of the imperial doctors. Further, Corvisart *père* thought that a good doctor had to be more than intelligent: he had to be bold. In his opinion, the older the physician became, the more skillful in equivocation he grew, so that great experience became an actual liability. Moreover, a staff of consultants deliberating as a committee, such as Napoleon III would have in 1870, could be paralyzed by conflicting views. Later on Léon Gambetta, suffering from appendicitis, remarked that if he were a simple worker he would be taken at once to a hospital, operated on, and possibly cured. Instead, a decision was postponed, and he died of a ruptured appendix.

To make matters worse, Napoleon III was a bad patient. He was hypersensitive to pain, as his doctors and his dentist all knew, though he bore pain with patience and real stoicism unless it was spontaneous and unexpected. The cutaneous neuralgia, for example, could drive him to extreme impatience. He was also inclined to hemorrhages and remembered several bad experiences after having had teeth extracted, once as a child and once in America, where he came briefly in 1837 after the Strasbourg fiasco. At that time an American surgeon told him that he did not know how to stop the flow of blood and that he would probably die. The dentist present then intervened and cauterized the wound. This episode left Napoleon with a durable faith in American dentists, though he thought the French variety were all charlatans.

Because the emperor thought that there must be an immediate cure or remedy for every ill, he was not only quick to reproach his physicians when they could not produce instant results, but vulnerable to the promises of quacks who would tend to belittle the skills of conventional medicine—and vulnerable to the advice of his ignorant and arrogant chief valet de chambre, Léon Cuxac, who evidently counseled the emperor to ignore the prescriptions of his physicians and had in their place a ready supply of ancestral remedies. The physicians could not obtain support through the Empress Eugénie, for she had as little faith in medicine and doctors as did the emperor. In any case, Dr. Conneau would probably not have confided in her, as he had a marked distaste for her; we can only guess that his dislike stemmed from his knowledge of the unhappy marriage, for he was always discreet. As Dr. Barthez said, it was a very difficult environment in which to practice medicine effectively. . . .

The array of Napoleon's ailments compels our sympathy as it becomes evident that he was rarely free of pain during most of his reign. It also becomes clear why his contemporaries, aware of his recurring distress, baffled by his methods of governance, astounded by the disasters which followed closely upon his triumphs, fell upon his illnesses as accountable for mysteries otherwise inexplicable. Moreover, an individual under the influence of an illness or a disease will seem to be altered, so that it is easy to assume that controversial or incorrect decisions have been the effect of disease. We all know of individuals whose behavior and judgment are deeply affected by ailments of even minor medical significance; history also knows of individuals, like Cardinal Richelieu for example, who suffered constantly, yet were not deflected from their courses nor displayed any flagging of their wills. The character of the afflicted individual, in other words, determines to a significant degree the effect disease has upon him.

The neurasthenia aside for a moment, the medical record of Napoleon fails entirely to provide substantial proof for a single example of a political decision that would have been made differently had the emperor been free of arthritis, gout, hemorrhoids, or the stone. Mistakes were made and policies went sour, but through it all and even after defeat we see his unswerving faith in the cause he represented, a gentle obstinacy. The decisions for peace in 1866 and for war in 1870 may remain forever controversial as to their wisdom, but neither was made hastily *nor by the emperor alone.* Good health would have been no guarantee of freedom from error, given the particular factors that determined those particular decisions.

On the other hand, the incompatibility of the imperial marriage did to an important degree affect the politics of the Second Empire. The emperor overcame the attacks of neurasthenia which threatened his stability in 1856 and learned to live with his marital disappointment, though we can hardly say that his subsequent amorous escapades were a satisfying substitute for the domestic bliss he had envisioned. From their alienation, however, grew the empress's determination to steer an independent political course. Though she had little to do with the formation of policies, she spoke about them freely, independently, and in ways that jeopardized their integrity. Without question she inadvertently misled the Austrians during the eighteen-sixties as to the emperor's real intentions and his capacity to govern. In 1870, as regent, she was only too willing to turn out the new liberal government whose prestige had been one of the major determinants in the decision to declare war, and her appraisal of the national crisis after the initial defeats prevented the retreat upon

Paris that Napoleon and MacMahon preferred and led straight to Sedan.

The intellectuals of the Second Empire, almost to the last man, were contemptuous of Napoleon III, believing him to be unspeakably mediocre. No one put that contempt more plainly than did Charles Baudelaire when he wrote that "Napoleon III's great claim to renown will have been that he showed how anybody at all, if only he gets hold of the telegraph and the printing-presses, can govern a great nation . . . and fame is the result of the matching of a personality with the national stupidity." Such hostility haunted the memory of the emperor for many decades after 1873, and only now, as we approach the centennial of his death, is it apparent that the passions have been withering and that a new Napoleon III has been emerging for some years. In his last will and testament, dated April 24, 1865, the emperor recommended that his son undertake a serious study of the acts and the writings of the "prisoner of St. Helena," but added advice that would not have come from St. Helena: "Power is a heavy burden. You cannot always do the good you would like to do, and your contemporaries are seldom fair. A man, therefore, must do his work and have faith in himself, a sense of his duty." The words for the son well serve the father.

II THE PROBLEMS OF THE TIMES

Domestic Policies

Frederick Arthur Simpson

THE ELECTION OF DECEMBER 10, 1848

Frederick Arthur Simpson (b. 1883), another Cambridge historian, may be considered the founder of the revisionist school in England. His two works, The Rise of Louis-Napoleon, 1808–1848 (London, 1909) and Louis-Napoleon and the Recovery of France, 1848–1856 (London, 1923), did much to counterbalance the earlier interpretations of such British critics of Napoleon III as Arthur William Kinglake. Simpson's careful scholarship and polished style give added weight to his attempt at rehabilitation. Without minimizing the importance of the Napoleonic legend, Simpson attributes Louis-Napoleon's election to a combination of equally important factors.

On November 4 the constitution was carried. On Sunday, the 12th, it was solemnly inaugurated at the Place de la Concorde. Mass was said by the new Archbishop of Paris, successor of him who had lost his life in a noble attempt to curtail the horrors of the June days. A *Te Deum* was sung, as for some especial mercy vouchsafed by heaven; symbolical figures of Peace and Plenty were there, as well as a plaster personification of the constitution itself. Incense rose in clouds from tripods at their feet to the tricolours above. The whole ceremony, if a little puerile, was more than a little pathetic. The bleak air of a dull November morning, slightly snowing on the assembled deputies, served to give an atmosphere of unreality to the rejoicings; while it emphasized, if it partly explained, the marked absence of any gathering of the people to witness the latest boon which was being conferred upon them. Indeed it was with ill-concealed relief that the country turned from the wrangling debates with which the constitution had been carried, and the mummery with which it had been inaugurated, to the practical and absorbing question which still remained to be decided. Who was to be the first president of the republic: In other words, was the republic to receive

From F. A. Simpson, *The Rise of Louis-Napoleon* (London, 1909). Reprinted by permission of Longmans, Green & Co., Limited.

the only direct sanction which the people had the opportunity of bestowing, namely, the election of a republican to the presidency?

It was soon evident that the presidency lay between Louis-Napoleon himself and General Cavaignac. The general had in his favor the memory of his service in June, the support of the Assembly, and—most important of all—the actual possession of power. But gratitude for his former services was by this time largely counteracted by irritation at his recent indiscretions; the Assembly was so unpopular in the country that its support was a very doubtful advantage; while even the army of functionaries, whose ready response to the voice of authority tells so much in France in favor of the existing power, even the *maires* and *préfets,* were beginning to grow restless under the uncertain hand of Cavaignac. The only assured following which remained to him in the country was the entire body of republican voters; but this force was numerically an unknown quantity. On the other hand, the general retained to the last one great and inalienable advantage over his opponent. By a clause in the constitution it was decided that, unless the successful candidate for the presidency obtained more than as many votes as all his opponents put together, the right of election would revert to the Assembly. And Cavaignac could absolutely depend upon the Assembly to elect himself. Thus he had a very substantial handicap in his favor; for if Louis-Napoleon obtained two votes for every one cast for Cavaignac, Cavaignac would still become President. There were several other candidates in the field who, though personally out of the running, were yet bound to be useful to the general. For their votes would count with his towards the total which Louis-Napoleon must more than surpass if he would become President.

On the face of it, then, Louis had an uphill task before him. But he too had in his favor many elements of success. In the first place, he had as sources of strength all that was complementary or contradictory to Cavaignac's. Thus, he was detested by the Assembly; but to be detested by a detested body is not to be oneself detested. Politically, the foes of our foes are our friends. Again, as section after section of the party of order was alienated by Cavaignac's ineptitude or offended by his indiscretions, each in turn rallied naturally to Cavaignac's principal opponent. And finally, the fact that Cavaignac was the official candidate of the republican party assured for Louis the support of the whole anti-republican feeling in the country.

Even more formidable were his positive sources of strength; his name, his career, and the monarchical instinct of the French people. Of these the first was the most important, for it carried with it all that shadowy transcendental heritage of which in our opening chapter we endeavored to give some idea. But it is a grave mistake —though a very common one—to assume that Louis-Napoleon's victory in 1848 was the triumph of a name alone. True, Louis without his name could have accomplished absolutely nothing. But this is not to say that the name without Louis could have effected absolutely everything, or indeed anything at all, in the region of practical politics. On the contrary, there is every reason to believe that had not Louis formulated into a definite creed the vague faith of which it was the symbol, had he not galvanized into substantive action the evasive life that was in it, had he not embodied it in concrete form and personified it in his individual existence—then the name of Napoleon would forever have lacked a local habitation; and that strange spirit which had risen from St. Helena, must have remained "a beautiful but ineffectual angel, beating in the void his luminous wings in vain." We may wish that it had been allowed so to remain; for in becoming effectual the angel ceased to be beautiful. Louis-Napoleon's faith in his star was about to be justified. But while it is doubtless good for a man "to hitch his waggon to a star," it is sometimes less good for the star. We may prefer that Niagara should continue to cast its waters in riotous and glorious waste; we may dislike to see it tamed by human intervention, and turned to servile uses. But though we grudge the engineer his triumph, we must still concede him such praise as is due to his ingenuity. After all, it is just because the process is artificial that we complain; and while we blame the workman for his interference, we cannot consistently deny the skill of his deed on the score that all that has been accomplished was automatic and inevitable.

How little the unaided name of Napoleon could have effected in 1848, we shall better understand if we glance for a moment at the position of the other bearers of that name. When the February revolution broke out, there was actually residing in France one surviving brother of the Emperor, Jerome, sometime king of Westphalia.

With him was his son, Prince Napoleon, who in form and feature bore striking resemblance to his great namesake. Yet they remained absolutely unnoticed. The Provisional Government never asked them to depart from Paris; it feared them as little as Louis-Philippe had feared them—Louis-Philippe who had contemptuously granted them the favor they asked of a return to France, and who at the time of his deposition was actually on the point of granting to this *fraterculus gigantis* a peerage and a pension. King Jerome was, and remained, a nonentity; Prince Napoleon, as soon as he ceased to be unknown, became intensely unpopular. When, after the establishment of the empire, Louis-Napoleon, before the birth of his son, adopted his cousin as his heir, he committed one of the most unpopular actions of his reign. An apologist who wished to defend this step could only do so by regarding it as a precaution against assassination; Charles the Second's remark to his brother might have been made by Louis-Napoleon to his cousin: "No one would kill me to make you king." The only other Napoleonic prince who appeared was Lucien's son Pierre, a turbulent and vicious vagabond who, like the rest of Lucien's sons, had been naturalized as a Roman citizen. Prince Napoleon was eccentric; the other Napoleonic princes with the exception of Louis himself were merely incompetent. But it was not their present lack of ability that nullified the advantage of their name: it was the fact that in the past they had one and all bartered or endeavored to barter away their birthright; and that not of their necessity for a morsel of meat, but that to their abundance they might add a bounty; readily foregoing their hope of a dynastic future for any handful of silver which Louis-Philippe might care to toss them in exchange for it.

Once in a moment of rare provocation Louis-Napoleon allowed himself to tax the nominal head of the Napoleonic house with this betrayal of the family cause. Stung by the ridicule which King Joseph had thrown on his Strasburg rising, he wrote to him in 1837: "Yes, my enterprise has failed. But it has made France hear that the family of the Emperor is not yet dead; that it can still count on the service of devoted friends; more, that its pretensions are not confined to the demand of petty pittances from the Government, but extend to the reconstruction in the people's cause of the fabric that foreigners and Bourbons have destroyed. This I have done; is it for you to cast it in my teeth?"

This was the mere truth. The other members of his family were living in placid or querulous retirement; at best their efforts were directed to the attainment by deferential behavior of some material benefit from the existing Government. Louis-Napoleon alone was sacrificing rest and fortune, was braving ridicule, danger, and discomfort in the faith of a dynastic future. Hence a path lay open to him in 1848 which was quite closed to any of them. For a birthright once sold is not easily recovered.

It is not, then, merely to their intrinsic interest that the circumstances of Louis-Napoleon's early life owe their claim to a somewhat detailed examination—though this narrative of them has failed in its purpose if they seem to lack such interest. Nor does their importance consist solely in a fact which would in itself suffice to render them important; that they served to mould and stamp with ineffaceable impress the character of a man who was for some fifteen years the most prominent figure in Europe. Their chief claim to the attention of the historian is after all this—not that they made Louis-Napoleon the kind of emperor he was, "a dreamer and a conspirator," but that without them he could scarcely have become emperor at all. In other words, without them there might have been no Second Empire. Even Louis-Napoleon, who was infinitely the cleverest representative of his name, could hardly have become president in 1848 without the advantage of his past career. While of the other members of the house it is not too much to say that even had they been endowed with all the advantages Louis had so laboriously acquired by eighteen years of labor, still they lacked the dexterity which alone enabled him to make full use of those advantages in 1848.

There remained a third factor in his success, which also has hardly been realized at its true value—the fact that at the time of the election to the presidency, the great majority of the French people desired nothing so much for the republic as its speedy and decent extinction. This is a fact which has been not merely ignored, but deliberately disguised, by many French historians of the Second Republic. There are many to whom the name of a republic has at all times a peculiar virtue; many who unconsciously hedge it about with a divinity no longer accorded to kings; so that while they regard with equanimity the fall of an unpopular monarchy, they condemn almost as an act of sacrilege the destruction of an unpopular republic. By such it is assumed that a republican form of government cannot but have an especial degree of popular approval. This would be in any case a dangerous assumption where the populace is instinctively monarchical; it becomes the height of unwisdom where revolutionary changes are the immediate result not of national movements, but of street-fighting in the capital. For in such cases when an existing government has been swept away by its own unpopularity, unless its opponents are agreed upon some immediate alternative to substitute for it, a republic automatically ensues. And since in Parisian revolution destruction is easier than construction, by far its easiest outcome is the one form of government which can be reached by a purely negative process. In fine, of governments in general in such a country as France, the republic is the one not least, but most likely to have a mere accident as its reason of existence.

But the history of the second French republic in particular has been invested with a wholly spurious pathos. Because it died young, therefore it was loved of the gods; because it was pitiful in its death, therefore it was delectable in its life; because the manner of its execution was illegal, unscrupulous, and indefensible, therefore its death sentence had not been plainly voted by the French people. To these sentimental non sequiturs other and more practical inducements were added. It was very natural that in the early days of the Third Republic its eulogists should tell it that it was the one form of government for which France had been pining for the better part of a century; that in 1830 and 1848 no less than in 1815 the country was balked of its wishes; that it needed the catastrophe of Sedan to give it what it had so long desired. But the Third Republic ought now to be able to dispense with help and defenders such as these; it should no longer need to rely on representations of the past which are as much a perversion of historical truth as those which came to the hand of Louis-Napoleon in the Napoleonic Legend. For, considering the relative possibilities of the two themes, the Second Republic has been as successfully idealized as the First Empire; and in one case, as in the other, historical criticism has been postponed to the interests of political propaganda.

Of all the diplomatic agents who were accredited to the Second Republic, there was none who objected more violently or more openly to the method by which it was finally suppressed than the British ambassador, Lord Normanby. Though not a republican, his detestation of the coup d'état was so unconcealed that it was found necessary to replace him by a less excitable successor. It may therefore be worth while to notice that however much he grudged Louis-Napoleon his success later, he clearly perceived in 1848 how greatly he was being served by the strength of the anti-republican feeling in France. Thus, towards the end of October, before the result of the election had become a foregone conclusion, he wrote that he considered Louis-Napoleon's election certain, "the persecution of the Government since February having identified his success with the overthrow of that of which the people had become so weary." This even more than the prestige of his name would win him support. A week later, discussing Cavaignac's chances, he adds, "The general opinion is that General Cavaignac's defeat is assured precisely on the ground on which he rests his hopes—that he is supposed specially identified with the republic." And on the morrow of the election he comments thus on Louis-Napoleon's overwhelming majority: "The memory of the Emperor is no doubt for something in this impulse, but the hatred of the Republic gives another signification to the name of Buonaparte, and the traditional recollection that it was by such means that the last republic was destroyed gives peculiar force to this mode of protestation."

On the eve of the elections, indeed, it became evident to the republicans themselves that France was not republican. Many of them confessed it openly; and if regard be paid to their admissions at the time itself, rather than to their memoirs and reminiscences published long afterwards with palpable political object, it is clear that they had already despaired of the republic before the result of the popular vote was made known. Almost alone among the republican leaders Cavaignac himself consistently and incessantly maintained in his every public utterance that the country was indeed republican. "The nation is seriously, unswervingly engaged to pursue the path of republicanism," he wrote in a public letter to General Changarnier in September. "To wish anything else would be to betray alike its interests and its wishes." It has generally been believed that such statements were made in all good faith; the transparent sincerity of the general has been contrasted with the subtle deceitfulness of his opponent. But it is worthy of note that Cavaignac himself, despite his public statements, was really perfectly well aware that the country was utterly opposed to republicanism. On

November 27 the general, in a confidential conversation, discussed his chances of success with the British ambassador. Normanby advised him not to appear to advocate the indefinite prolongation of the present unpopular assembly. "The general's only answer was that new elections for some time to come would destroy the republic. I said: 'Then you do not think the country republican?' 'Certainly not,' was his answer, 'and never was, and never was.' 'And you expect to make it so?' 'It is with that object alone that I seek the presidency.'" In other words, Cavaignac confessed that he was seeking the presidency with the intention of riveting upon the people a form of government which he knew they did not desire, but to which he hoped in time to accustom them. Louis-Napoleon was seeking it with the intention of freeing them from a form of government of which, like Cavaignac, he knew they wished to be rid, and of giving them one which he really believed they desired. That his ambition was the more personal one, is true; that his method of accomplishing his object was illegal, and worse than illegal, cannot be denied. But if we turn from the means employed to the ends in view, his was perhaps not so very much less legitimate than his opponent's.

It is difficult in regard to the election itself to find any great distinction between the methods adopted by the two candidates. The Bonapartist papers contained violent and unfair attacks on Cavaignac; those which supported Cavaignac contained equally abusive and unfair attacks upon Louis-Napoleon. If the prince's agents distributed flattering portraits of him, his opponents were no less prodigal of scandalous caricatures. If his supporters availed themselves to the full of the grievances which can be ranged against any existing power, yet the Government unhesitatingly attempted to bring all the great influence of existing power to bear against their antagonist. "I cannot doubt that the most unscrupulous use will be made of the powers which centralisation has put into the hands of the Government to influence the result," wrote Normanby on November 2. On that day a circular was issued to the prefects, directing them to impress upon their subordinates the real interests of the republic. While the Minister of the Interior explained their duties to the prefects, the Minister of Education reminded the schoolmasters that a fund of over a million francs voted them by the Assembly was about to be distributed; gratitude either for past or future favors should make them good republicans. Cavaignac himself attempted by tardy activities and civilities to propitiate some of the several sections of society which he had contrived to offend. The general was indeed an ideally bad candidate. Not greatly caring if he were disapproved, he disliked and resented the necessity of being "on approval." Personally disinclined to make use of his official powers in his own favor, he did not intervene decidedly to prevent his colleagues from using pressure on his behalf. He had thus the appearance of doing hesitatingly what it would greatly have profited him to do with vigor, and greatly have honored him to leave undone altogether. By this course he sacrificed at once the moral prestige of a dignified reserve, and the material benefit which must have resulted from an unblushing exercise of official pressure.

Towards the end of November he achieved his last public triumph. Many had complained, with reason, of his conduct of affairs since June; it was reserved for a few of the least scrupulous of his opponents to attack him for his actual use of his dictatorship in that month. It was asserted that he had purposely allowed the rising to attain its actual proportions, in order to render his own dictatorship inevitable. On November 25 he answered this charge in the Chamber. There could be no doubt as to the result of a defense made in the one place where his influence was unshaken, on the one point on which his conduct was unassailable; by an overwhelming majority the deputies reaffirmed the vote they had passed on the morrow of the civil war—that General Cavaignac had deserved well of his country.

But by this time it was clear to everyone that the country would have none of him. On the very eve of the elections, by a last act of folly his Government renewed the fears of the supporters of order, by including in a list of political pensioners the heirs of several of Louis-Philippe's would-be assassins, among them those of that very Fieschi into whose cell Louis-Napoleon had been thrust after Boulogne. The list was withdrawn and cancelled almost immediately, but the impression it created could not be effaced.

Five days later, on December 10, the election took place. Although it was known almost directly that Louis-Napoleon had received the necessary majority, it was not until the 20th that the result was officially announced. Nearly five and a half millions of votes were given in favor of Louis; less than one and a half to the official republican candidate, Cavaignac. The other four candidates did not gain half-a-million votes between them; Lamartine, the eloquent defender of the popular vote, obtained from it less than eighteen thousand supporters.

It was on the evening of the 20th that the result of the vote was announced in the Chamber. Cavaignac resigned his powers; the president of the Assembly announced that Louis-Napoleon Bonaparte was duly elected to the presidency. Then in the dimly-lighted Chamber Louis-Napoleon himself came forward to the tribune—dressed as on another occasion in black, and bearing on his breast the grand cross of the Legion of Honor which he had worn at his trial before the Court of Peers. He took the oath of fidelity to the republic prescribed by the Constitution, and then amid profound silence he made a short speech in which he expressed in modest language his hope that in conjunction with the Assembly he might be able to found a republic at once just and democratic, neither visionary nor reactionary in its behavior. Then, accompanied by one or two friends, and escorted by a few officials, he left the Chamber and proceeded to the palace of the Elysée where a few rooms had been hastily prepared for his use. There that evening he gave his first small dinner-party as President; and his guests were his companions in those mad invasions of Strasburg and Boulogne: Vaudrey and Laity, Bataille, Mocquard and Persigny. What toasts were drunk that night we do not know: but some at least who drank them must have let their thoughts range on; from the delights of old battles which though lost were yet won, to the sterner satisfaction of new conflicts still untried.

Karl Marx

THE EIGHTEENTH BRUMAIRE OF LOUIS BONAPARTE

Karl Marx (1818–1883) needs no introduction to students of modern European history. First published in 1852, The Eighteenth Brumaire of Louis Bonaparte *was second only to Victor Hugo's* Napoléon le Petit *in shaping up the image of Napoleon III, "the Hero Crapulinsky," as a feeble caricature of his uncle. In the following selection Marx explains Louis-Napoleon's election and the consolidation of his personal power in terms of the contemporaneous structure of French society. According to him, the conservative, ignorant, petty peasant-proprietors who made up the bulk of population provided Louis-Napoleon with a broad base of support.*

Just as the Bourbons were the dynasty of the great landlords, and just as the July monarchy was the dynasty of money, so the Bonapartes are the dynasty of the peasants, the small holders who form the bulk of the French population. Not the Bonaparte who threw himself at the feet of the bourgeois parliament, but the Bonaparte who gave the bourgeois parliament the key of the street, is the chosen of the peasantry. For three years, the towns had been able to falsify the significance of the election of December 10th, and to cheat the peasants of their desire, the restoration of the Empire. The purpose of the election of December 10, 1848, was not achieved until the coup d'état of December 2nd, 1851.

The peasants who farm their own small holdings form the majority of the French population. Throughout the country, they live in almost identical conditions, but enter very little into relationships with one another. Their mode of production isolates them, instead of bringing them into mutual contact. The isolation is intensified by the inadequacy of the means of communication in France, and by the poverty of the peasants. Their farms are so small that there is practically no scope for a division of labor, no opportunity for scientific agriculture. Among the peasantry, therefore, there can be no multiplicity of development, no differentiation of talents, no wealth of social relationships. Each family is almost self-sufficient, producing

From Karl Marx, *The Eighteenth Brumaire of Louis Bonaparte* (New York, 1926). Reprinted by permission of International Publishers. Translated by Eden & Cedar Paul.

on its own plot of land the greater part of its requirements, and thus providing itself with the necessaries of life through an inter-change with nature rather than by means of intercourse with society. Here is a small plot of land, with a peasant farmer and his family; there is another plot of land, another peasant with wife and children. A score or two of these atoms make up a village, and a few score of villages make up a department. In this way, the great mass of the French nation is formed by the simple addition of like entities, much as a sack of potatoes consists of a lot of potatoes huddled into a sack. Insofar as millions of families live in economic circum-stances which distinguish their mode of life, their interests, and their culture, from those of other classes, and make them more or less hostile to other classes, these peasant families form a class. But insofar as the tie between the peasants is merely one of pro-pinquity, and insofar as the identity of their interests has failed to find expression in a community, in a national association, or in a political organization, these peasant families do not form a class. They are, therefore, unable to assert their class interests in their own name, whether through parliament or through a congress. They cannot represent themselves, and must be represented. He who is to be their representative must also appear to them as their lord and master, as one holding authority over them, one wielding un-restricted governmental powers, who will protect them against the other classes, and who will send them the rain and the sunshine from above. Consequently, the political influence of the peasants finds its last expression in an executive which subordinates society to its own autocratic will.

Historical tradition had nourished among the French peasants the superstition that a man named Napoleon would return in the fulness of time bringing them all that their hearts could desire. Lo, there came one giving himself out as this Messiah. He bore the name of Napoleon, and, by the terms of the Code Napoléon, *la recherche de la paternité est interdite*. After twenty years' vaga-bondage and a number of preposterous adventures, this man be-comes Emperor of the French. The prophecy has brought its own fulfilment. The nephew's fixed idea has been realized because it coincides with the fixed idea of the peasant class, the majority of the French nation.

Here a critic may exclaim: "But what about the peasant risings in many parts of France, the dragooning of the peasants by the army; the imprisonment and transportation of large numbers of peasants?"

It is true that France has known no such widespread persecution of the peasantry "for demagogic intrigues," since the days of Louis XIV. Let there be no misunderstanding here. The Bonaparte dynasty does not represent the revolutionary peasant, but the conservative peasant. It does not represent those among the peasantry who wish to escape from the narrow confines of their farming life; it represents those who wish to perpetuate and consolidate these conditions. It does not represent that part of the rural population which, instinct with energy, wishes to join forces with the townsfolk for the overthrow of the old order. On the contrary, it represents those who, hidebound in their conservatism, are resolute champions of the old order, and who look to the ghost of the Napoleonic Empire to save and to favor themselves and their petty farms. It does not represent the enlightenment of the peasants, but their superstition; not their judgment, but their prejudices; not their future, but their past; not the reincarnation of Cévennes, but the reincarnation of Vendée.

The three-years' rule of the parliamentary republic had freed some of the French peasants from the Napoleonic illusion, and had even revolutionized them, though superficially; but the bourgeoisie had forcibly repressed any attempt on their part to advance. Under the parliamentary republic there was a struggle between the modern and the traditional consciousness of the French peasantry. This struggle took the form of incessant warfare between the schoolmasters and the priests. The bourgeoisie took the side of the priests. The peasants had made a first attempt to maintain their own independence against governmental authority. This was shown in the protracted conflict between the mayors and the prefects. The bourgeoisie deposed recalcitrant mayors. Finally, during the regime of the parliamentary republic, the peasants of various regions had risen against their own offspring, the army. The bourgeoisie had punished them with states of siege and with distraints upon their goods. Now this same bourgeoisie complains bitterly of the stupidity of the masses, of the "vile multitude" which has betrayed it to Bonaparte. The bourgeoisie had itself forcibly strengthened the imperialist sentiment of the peasantry by maintaining the conditions under which this peasant religion came into existence. What can the bourgeoisie do but dread the stupidity of the masses while they remain conservative, and the enlightened understanding of the masses as soon as they become revolutionary?

In the risings that followed the coup d'état, some of the peasants were making an armed protest against their own votes on December 10, 1848. Their schooling since then has taught them sense. But they had signed a covenant with the underworld of history, and history held them to their bond. Most of the peasants were still so steeped in prejudice that in the Reddest departments they were most frank and enthusiastic in their support of Bonaparte. In their view, the National Assembly had restricted their freedom of movement, and now they were merely breaking the fetters which the towns had imposed upon the will of the countryside. In some places, they even entertained the grotesque fancy that a revolutionary Convention might exist side by side with a Napoleon!

By the first revolution, serfdom was completely abolished, and the peasants became freeholders. Then came Napoleon, who confirmed and regulated the conditions on which they could exploit their newly acquired farms and enjoy the freshly won sense of ownership. But that is the very thing which now bears so hardly on the peasant, this system of petty proprietorship, this parcelling out of the land into small privately owned plots, a system consolidated in France under the Napoleonic regime. It was the material conditions of existence, the system of land tenure and the associated method of agricultural production, which converted the serf of feudal days into a small freeholder and made Napoleon Emperor. Two generations have been enough to produce the inevitable result; the progressive deterioration of agriculture and the increasing indebtedness of the tillers of the soil. The "Napoleonic" land tenure, which in the opening years of the nineteenth century enfranchised and enriched the French countryfolk, has by the middle of the same century enslaved and pauperized them. But this very system of peasant landholdings is the first of the *idées napoléoniennes* which the second Napoleon must perforce uphold. If, in common with the peasants, he still clings to the illusion that the cause of their ruin is to be sought, not in the system of petty proprietorship itself, but elsewhere, in secondary external conditions, his experiments will burst like soap-bubbles when they come into contact with the actual conditions of production.

By the economic development of this smallholding system, the relationship between the peasantry and the other classes of society has been turned upside down. Under the first Napoleon, the parcelling out of the land encouraged free competition in the rural districts, and favored the beginnings of great industry in the towns. The peasant class was an embodied and ubiquitous protest against the landed aristocracy, so recently overthrown. The roots which the new system of smallholding struck deep into French soil, cut off the supply of nutriment upon which feudalism had depended. The landmarks of peasant proprietorship were the natural fortifications of the bourgeoisie against any attempt at a coup de main that might be made by the old overlords. But in the course of the nineteenth century, the feudal extortioner was replaced by the urban usurer; the obligations that the feudal system had imposed upon those who were bound to the soil found their modern counterparts in the obligations to the mortgagee; aristocratic landlordism had been exchanged for bourgeois capitalism. The peasant's holding is still only the pretext whereby the capitalist is enabled to draw profit, interest, and rent from the land, while leaving the cultivator to wrest his own wages from the soil. French agricultural land is so heavily burdened with mortgages, that the interest paid on them is equal to the interest on the British national debt. The system of petty proprietorship, inevitably resulting in this enslavement to capital, has transformed the mass of the French nation into troglodytes. Sixteen million peasants (the women and children included) live in cavelike hovels, most of which have but one opening, though some have two, and the most favored ones, three. Now, windows are to a house what the five senses are to the head. At the beginning of the century, the bourgeois system of society, placed the State as sentinel in front of the newly-created petty landholdings, and manured their soil with laurels. Today, that same bourgeois system has become a vampire which sucks the blood and marrow from the peasants' little farms, and throws them into the alembic of capital. The Code Napoléon is now nothing more than the warrant for distraints and forced sales. According to official figures, there are in France four million paupers, vagabonds, criminals, and prostitutes. Next come five millions (always including women and children) living on the very margin of subsistence, now in the country, and now, with their rags and their children, migrating for a time to the towns. The result is that the interests of the peasants no longer coincide, as during the reign of the first Napoleon, with the interests of the bourgeoisie, with the interests of capital. There is now a conflict of interests. The peasants, therefore, find their natural allies and leaders in the urban proletariat, whose mission it is to subvert the bourgeois order of society. But the mission of the strong, the absolutist government of Louis Bonaparte (and here we have the second *idée napoléonienne)* is the forcible defense of this "material order." That is why the catchword *"ordre matériel"* finds a place in all Bonaparte's proclamations against the turbulent peasants.

Mortgages are not the only burdens imposed by capital upon the smallholder. There is also the burden of taxation. Taxes form the vital sustenance of the bureaucracy, the army, the clergy, and the court—in a word of the whole executive apparatus. Strong government and crushing taxation are identical. From its very nature, the system of petty proprietorship is a suitable standing ground for an all-powerful and numberless bureaucracy. It brings about an equable levelling of conditions and personalities throughout the country, thus facilitating the exercise of an even influence upon all parts of this homogeneous mass, an influence emanating from a central point. It destroys the aristocratic gradations between the masses of the people and the State authority. Consequently, it calls for the universal and direct intervention of this governmental authority and its instruments. Finally, the system produces an unemployed excess of population, consisting of persons for whom there is no productive occupation either upon the land or in the towns, and who therefore reach out their hands towards the civil service as a sort or respectable alms-giving institution, and do their utmost to multiply the number of official posts. The first Napoleon, opening new markets at the point of the bayonet, and plundering the whole continent of Europe, was able to repay with interest what he extorted by taxation. Then, taxation was a spur to peasant industry; now, it robs that industry of its last support, and opens the door to pauperism. Indeed, a huge bureaucracy, well-fed and well-dressed, is, of all the *idées napoléoniennes,* the one which best suits the requirements of the second Bonaparte. How could it be otherwise, seeing that he is forced to create, side by side with the genuine classes of society, an artificial caste to which the maintenance of his regime becomes a bread-and-butter question? That was why one of the first financial operations was the raising of official salaries to their old level, and the creation of new sinecures.

Another *idée napoléonienne* is the rule of the priests as an instrument of government. But whereas at the outset the peasant smallholders, being in harmony with society, dependent upon natural forces, and subject to an authority which protected them from on high, were naturally religious—nowadays, when they are burdened with debt, at odds with society and authority, and forced out of their old rut, they are naturally irreligious. Heaven was a pleasing accessory to the newly-won plot of farming land, all the more since rain and sunshine come from heaven; but to offer heaven in exchange for a landholding is an insult. In the light of such an offer, the priest can only be regarded as the anointed bloodhound of the earthly police—yet another *idée napoléonienne!* The next expedition against Rome will take place within the frontiers of France, but it will be of the opposite kind to that of Monsieur de Montalembert.

Finally, the culminating point of the *idées napoléoniennes* is the preponderance of the army. To the peasant proprietors, the army was the *point d'honneur*. It was themselves transformed into heroes, defending their newly-acquired property in foreign campaigns, glorifying their recently won nationality, plundering and revolutionizing the world. The uniform was their gala dress; war was their poetry; the plot of land, imaginatively magnified and rounded off, was the fatherland; and patriotism was an idealized sense of ownership. But the enemies against whom the French peasant has now to defend his property are no longer Cossacks; they are bailiffs and tax-gatherers. The holdings are no longer in the so-called fatherland; they are in the register of mortgages! Even the army, now, has ceased to consist of the flower of the peasant youth; it is recruited from among the rank, weedy growths of the rural slum proletariat. A large proportion of these recruits are *remplaçants,* substitutes, just as the second Bonaparte is himself a mere *remplaçant,* a substitute for Napoleon. The heroic feats of this army take the form of raids on the peasantry, of police duties. When the internal contradictions of his system drive the chief of the Society of December the Tenth into exile, his army, after a few acts of brigandage, will earn for itself, not laurels, but hard knocks.

We see, then, that all the *idées napoléoniennes* are the ideas of the petty proprietors in their callow youth. When the peasants have grown old and experienced, these ideas seem nonsensical to them. In the death struggle of the system of petty proprietorship, the Napoleonic ideas have become hallucinations; the words are empty phrases; the spirits are but ghosts. Yet the parody of Empire was necessary that the mass of the French nation might be freed from the yoke of tradition, and that the opposition between the State authority and society might be displayed in all its nudity. With the progressive decay of the system of petty proprietorship, the State structure that was founded upon it collapses. The governmental centralization indispensable to modern society can rise only upon the ruins of the militarist and bureaucratic governmental machinery which was created as a counterblast to feudalism.

The conditions of peasant life in France are the solution of the riddle of the general elections of December 20th and 21st, which carried the second Bonaparte to the top of Mount Sinai—not to receive laws, but to give them.

Obviously, now, the bourgeoisie had no alternative. It had perforce to vote for Bonaparte. At the Council of Constance, when the puritans complained of the dissolute lives of the popes, and wailed about the need for moral reform, Cardinal d'Ailly thundered in reply: "Only the devil in person can save the Catholic Church, and you are asking for angels!"

In like manner, after the coup d'état, the French bourgeoisie exclaimed: "Only the chief of the Society of December the Tenth can save capitalist society. Nothing but theft can save property; nothing but perjury can save religion; nothing but bastardy can save the family; nothing but disorder can save order!" Bonaparte as a self-appointed autocrat, regards the safeguarding of "bourgeois order" as his mission. But the main prop of the bourgeois order is the middle class. He looks upon himself, therefore, as the representative of the middle class, and issues his decrees in this sense. Nevertheless, he is himself only a power in so far as he has broken the political power of the middle class, and daily breaks it anew. Consequently, he looks upon himself as the adversary of the political and literary power of the middle class. Yet insofar as he protects the material power of that class, he continually recreates its political power. His aim must be to keep the cause in being, while he shuffles the effect out of the world. But this cannot be achieved without some slight confounding of cause and effect, at the point where the two, in their interaction, lose their distinctive characteristics. That is why he issues new decrees which smudge the boundary line. At the same time, Bonaparte feels himself to be the representative of the peasantry, and of the people in general, as against the bourgeoisie; he regards himself as the man who is to bring happiness to the lower classes, and to do so within the framework of bourgeois society. To this end, he issues more decrees, which are to forestall the "true socialists," and steal the socialist thunder. Above all, however, Bonaparte looks upon himself as the chief of the Society of December the Tenth, as representative of the slum proletariat, to which he himself, his entourage, his government, and his army belong. (We must not forget that the main object of the slum proletariat is to seek its own advantage and to draw Californian prizes out of the State treasury.) He consolidates his position as chief of the Society of December the Tenth, with decrees, without decrees, and in spite of decrees.

These contradictions in the man's mission explain the contradictions in his government. That is why his government alternately seeks to win and then to humiliate this class or that, and ends by arraying all classes against itself, so that the actual insecurity of the government forms a ludicrous contrast to its hectoring tones and dictatorial methods—which the nephew has carefully copied from the uncle.

Industry and commerce, the business affairs of the middle class, are to thrive as if in a hothouse under this "strong government." Numberless railway concessions are granted. But the Bonapartist slum proletariat must feather its nest. Those in the know, play hanky panky on the Stock Exchange with the railway concessions. No capital is forthcoming for the railways. The Bank of France must undertake to advance money upon railway shares. At the same time, money must be made out of the bank, and so the bank has to be cajoled. It is released from the obligation to publish weekly reports. The government comes to an agreement with the bank, and the government is to get the lion's share of the spoils. Work must be found for the common people. State undertakings are inaugurated. The State undertakings must be financed, and that will tend to increase taxation. This can be avoided by an attack upon the national bondholders, by a reduction of the interest on the national debt from 5 per cent to 4½ per cent. In return for this, the middle class must have a sop. Let us double the wine tax for the lower orders, who buy *en détail,* and halve the wine tax for members of the middle class who drink *en gros.* Genuine labor organizations are to be dissolved, but there is a promise of miracles to be worked by labor organization at some future day. The peasants must be given a helping hand. Let us found mortgage banks, which will intensify the burden of peasant debt and accelerate the concentration of property. But these banks must be turned to special account in squeezing money out of the confiscated estates of the House of Orleans. No capitalist will lend his aid to the latter part of the scheme, which is not mentioned in the decree. The result is that the mortgage banks exist only on paper. And so on; and so on.

Bonaparte would fain pose as the patriarchal benefactor of all classes. But he cannot give to one class without robbing the others. In the days of the Fronde, it was said of the Duke of Guise that he was the most obliging man in France, seeing that he had transformed all his possessions into his partisans' obligations towards himself. In like manner, Bonaparte would fain be the most obliging man in France, and would gladly transform all the property and all the labor of France into a personal obligation towards himself. He would like to steal the whole of France in order to make a present of the stolen goods to France, or, rather, in order to buy France anew with French money—for in the role of chief of the Society of December the Tenth he is compelled to buy that which ought to belong to him. All State institutions—the Senate, the Council of State, the legislature, the Legion of Honor, the soldiers' medals, the public baths and washhouses, the State buildings, the railways, the *état-major* of the National Guard (to the exclusion of the privates), and the confiscated estates of the House of Orleans—all are to be transformed into an Institute for Purchase and Sale. Every post in the army and in the governmental machine is to become a means for money-making. But the most important feature of the process, in which France is to be annexed in order to be given back to herself, are the percentages which will accrue to the head and the members of the Society of December the Tenth. Countess L., the Duke of Morny's mistress, wittily characterized the confiscation of the estates of the House of Orleans in the phrase *"C'est le premier vol de l'aigle!"* The witticism applies to all the flights of this eagle, which is, in reality, far more like a crow. Like the Carthusian monk in the legend, admonishing the miser who made a boastful display of the wealth on which he expected to live for many years to come, Bonaparte and his henchmen say to themselves daily: *"Tu fai conto sopra i bene, bisogna prima far il conto sopra gli anni."*[1] Lest they should make any mistake in reckoning up the years, they reckon up the minutes. At the court, in the ministerial offices, at the head of the administration and the army, we see a crowd of fellows, of which the best that can be said is that no one knows whence it hails. They form a noisy, disreputable rabble, eager for loot. In their fine uniforms, decked with gold lace, they look as grotesque as the dignitaries of Emperor Soulouque. My readers will be able to form a picture of this upper stratum of the Society of December the Tenth when they realize that Véron-Crevel is their moralist, and that Granier de Cassagnac is their thinker. Guizot, in the days when he was Prime Minister, had employed Granier de Cassagnac on the staff of a petty newspaper intended to counteract the influence of the legitimist opposition, and had been wont to say of his tool: *"C'est le roi des drôles."* When we contemplate the court and the kin of Louis Bonaparte, we do wrong if our thoughts turn back to the days of the Regency or to those of the reign of Louis XV. Let us remember the words of Madame Girardin. Many times ere this, France has been under the rule of kept women, but, never before under the rule of kept men.

Harassed by the conflicting demands of his situation, forced like a conjurer to rivet public attention upon himself as substitute of the first Napoleon, compelled every day to carry out a miniature coup d'état, Bonaparte throws the whole bourgeois economy into confusion, lays sacrilegious hands on everything which the revolution of 1848 had regarded as sacred, makes some tolerant of revolution and others eager for revolution, and generates anarchy in the name of order. Through his deeds, the State machine is robbed of all sublimity, is profaned, is made both loathsome and ridiculous. The cult of the Holy Coat of Treves is transferred to Paris, where it becomes the cult of the Napoleonic imperial mantle. But if the imperial mantle should, in the end, fall upon the shoulders of Louis Bonaparte, the iron statue of Napoleon will crash from the top of the Vendôme column.

---

[1] "You are counting upon your goods, but you would do better, first, to count upon your years"; i.e. you can't depend upon living long enough to enjoy your hoarded wealth.—Ed.

Henri Guillemin

THE COUP D'ÉTAT OF DECEMBER 2, 1851

Henri Guillemin (b. 1903), a Normalien and a Doctor of Letters, left the teaching profession at the end of World War II to follow a diplomatic career. A prolific writer, he is best known for his studies of Lamartine and other nineteenth-century literary figures. Le coup du 2 décembre, from which this selection is taken, and his other works on Napoleon III and the Second Empire place him squarely in the anti-revisionist camp. In fact, the righteous indignation with which Guillemin approaches his subject is matched only by Victor Hugo's.

Let us consider in its historical context the tremendous revolution carried out by Louis-Napoleon "with the speed of lightning and the daring of an eagle" (to borrow a phrase from Amédée de Céséna).

First, we have a man full of dreams, desires, and tricks; a man fortunate enough to bear the name of Bonaparte, although his father was probably a Dutchman. He grew up in a German atmosphere, and was a captain of artillery in Switzerland and a "constable" in England. He spoke with a German accent and affected the phlegm of an Englishman. He was determined to use his name to make his fortune. His needs were immoderate and his wants unlimited. He simply wanted everything.

He was far from unintelligent, and had once liked to toy with ideas. But now, passed forty, at once sensuous and realistic, he no longer possessed even the semblance of a doctrine. The dreams of yesteryears had been replaced by a passion for scheming. He preferred the gratification of his lusts to the formulation of concepts. As he advanced toward his self-assigned goal, the complete control of government and absolute power over France, he himself perhaps did not realize the extent to which he was seeking, not the role of a great statesman, far from it, but merely the pleasures of high life.

Second, we find a small team of men, who had cast their lot with this Louis Bonaparte. Some, like Persigny, were long-time followers; others, like Morny, rather contemptuous at first, had recently revised their estimates of his chances. Morny was not his half-brother for

From Henri Guillemin, *Le coup du 2 décembre* (Paris, 1951). © Editions Gallimard, 1951. Editor's translation.

nothing. Equally fond of money and pleasure, both men were most eager "to lay their hands on the revenues of the state." As Odilon Barrot rightly said: "The coup d'état was carried out for the benefit of one man and one family [clan would be a better term]. History will record this truth." But there was more to it than that. The truth "recorded by history" was that the coup d'état would never have succeeded without the complicity of a whole class. The gangsters of the Elysée would have been powerless had not the men of property, who certainly recognized them for the blackmailers that they were, deemed that they alone could provide what the monied classes had been seeking since February, 1848: a strong government, capable of shoring up the shaken foundations of society. In other words, a government that would guarantee the obedient silence and the cheap labor of the proletariat, whose function it was to provide them with their wealth.

The coup d'état of December 2nd was the sequel and the natural outcome of the June days. This cardinal fact throws light on a whole chapter of our history. Calling for a "Roman Expedition at home" to crush the French Republic, Montalembert declared, on May 22, 1850, that "it was imperative to continue and to win the battle of June, 1848." In the September 29, 1849, issue of the *Univers,* Veuillot looked for a way "to prevent the threatening storm which the guns of June have failed to dissipate." On the morrow of the coup d'état, he explained to Foisset why one and all should rally behind Louis Bonaparte and vote *yes* in the plebiscite: "The revolution of December 2nd was a true counterrevolution. It represents an even greater step forward than June 24, 1848."

Even though he sensed the preparation of a presidential plot backed by the army, Lamartine could not bring himself to believe in "a revolution by the soldiery," because it would heap so much dishonor on France. He labelled such an eventuality as "treasonable, cowardly, and bestial." Treasonable, because the President would have "to turn against the country, the sword pledged to defend its institutions." Cowardly, because force would be used against naked laws and a trusting people. Bestial, because unlike the revolutions of 1789, 1830, and 1848, which were expressions of a longing for greater justice, this one would amount to no more than a rogue's crime, a highway robbery. Lamartine further believed that this "revolution without an ideal," this "sordid coup," would be all the more hideous because it would not even arouse the enthusiasms once generated by the glory-covered man of 18th Brumaire. Another observer, Hübner, was to remark on December 5: "The bourgeoisie won in July, 1830; the people in February, 1848; the army on December 3, 1851. One might think we were in Mexico." Lamartine and Hübner were right. What we have here is indeed a barracks' plot. Seduced by the prospect of emerging as the masters of France, a number of generals, hiding behind a civilian, joined in a most fruitful operation. Captain Hippolyte de Mauduit, who eulogized the coup d'état, loyally entitled his book *The Military Revolution of December 2nd.* But Mauduit, Hübner, and Lamartine forgot to mention the essential fact: the constabularies and generals of December 2nd were the agents and the henchmen of a class that had assigned them the task of assuring order and security.

In February, 1848, the emergence of an aroused proletariat, vocal in its demands for full emancipation, had been viewed by the propertied classes as a danger and a scandal. As soon as they were in a position to do so, they had taught these troublemakers "a lesson." Theirs was the reflex of a wild beast defending its prey. These people "who seek happiness at our expense" (thus, Montalembert) had to be made aware of the penalties to be exacted on anyone who threatened, not the lives, thank heaven for that, but the position of the propertied classes. Up to that time, the notables, most of whom were totally ignorant of the indescribable living conditions of the working classes, had never questioned the righteousness of the established order. At one and the same time, they were confronted with the loss or a drastic reduction of the profits accruing to them in a system which they had hitherto considered unassailable, and they were awakened to the plight of the proletariat by the works of such "respectable" writers as Adolphe Blanqui, member of the Institute. No longer sure of themselves, they became ugly. A reign of terror appeared to them as the sole means of salvation. Turn the state into a terrifying institution; let it impose on the workers the unconditional acceptance of the order which they had dared to challenge. As Proudhon had warned: "So long as society operates on an unregulated economy, there will inevitably be exploiters and exploited, and a strong power to protect the parasites." What was needed, then, was the tutelar tyranny for which Doudan was clamoring; a rich man's police state apt to make the poor cower.

The men of the Party of Order thus set out in search of a "man with a whip," who would set things right by relegating the workers to their proper place in society. "Admonished by the clergy, watched by the army, frightened by the judiciary, and owned by the feudal lords of capitalism and commerce" (to quote Proudhon again), the proletarians would resume their natural function as producers of wealth. The important thing was to assure the "immediate and lasting victory of order," to bring back the happy days when one could live "in complete security." The idea was not only to cut the people's fever, as in 1848, but to stamp out any future source of infection.

Cavaignac first loomed up as the possible savior. The bloodletting of June was to his credit, and Doudan expressed the pious hope that he might permanently consolidate his position as "king of the scarecrows." Unfortunately, he was soon to prove a disappointment. His old enemy, Marshal Bugeaud, tersely commented that he was "a cow in a hyena's skin." The Marshal, who was noted for his bravado, next emerged as a distinct possibility. But his appeals for "moderation" showed him to be a weakling. As if it were a time for compromise! Only the naive mourned him when he died unexpectedly. What about Changarnier? For a few months all hopes centered on him. Doudan begged him repeatedly to remain in the saddle and to keep his guns at the ready. Veuillot noted that his very name terrorized the *montagnards*. The Conservatives waited in vain for him to make an overture.

As Maupas was later to write in his *Mémoires*: "The men of the Party of Order wanted a coup d'état before, and just as much as we did. They failed to attempt it themselves because they lacked resolution and confidence." Nothing could be truer. The deputies of the Party of Order were nostalgic for that golden age (why, it was only yesterday!) when there were no "social questions," no proletariat, no squabbles over hours and wages. They worked for a royalist restoration that would turn the clock back to these happy days. This time, however, the King would be given full powers. Unfortunately for them, they could not agree when it came to the choice of the future sovereign. Some favored Henri V, the pretender of the senior branch; others backed the Comte de Paris, the claimant of the junior branch. The latter was too young to rule, and the prospects of a regency weakened his candidacy. Although Changarnier had been ready to

take power since December, 1848, he never made a move because
he was held back by the watchful and rival clans of the Orleanists
and Legitimists, uncertain as they were for whom this "sphinx with
a whig" proposed to act.

The proponents of immediate action became impatient with all
this wavering. Even while the various factions continued jockeying
for position, the disease spread and republicanism made some gains
among the masses. The elections of May, 1849, were a fiasco.
Almost two hundred Republicans were elected! Unless something
drastic was done, the elections of May, 1852, promised to be even
worse. It was imperative that they should not be held—at least not
under a franchise giving an equal voice to rich and poor. The wisest
and most clear-minded men saw only one way out: the Czar and the
Cossacks as in 1815. Foreign intervention may have been a bitter
pill to swallow, but there were no practicable alternatives. Morny
calmly explained this to Madame de Flahaut on May 16, 1849.
Romieu also placed his hopes on "Russian guns." To Proudhon, the
politicians of the Rue de Poitiers were but "the welcoming escort
of the Russians on the road to Paris."

In this favorable climate, Louis Bonaparte meticulously laid his
plans. His task was to present himself as preferable to these distant
and not quite satisfactory saviors. He was willing and on the spot.
Anyone ready to take him seriously and to trust him must immediately realize that he was better fitted than anybody to give complete
satisfaction. It took the Right some time to recognize him for what
he was: the one indispensable man. Little by little, the more perspicacious conservatives came to look upon him as worthy of consideration. The Rue de Poitiers had endorsed his candidacy in
December, 1848, as something of a joke and with secret contempt.
This needy, unlucky adventurer, overfond of women and horses,
whom Thiers had further labelled as "stupid," had simply happened
to be in the right place at the right time. To elevate this idiot to the
Presidency of the Republic had just the right touch; it was a good
trick to play on an execrable regime. "Prince Louis'" regime would
merely serve as a link toward a royalist restoration. But, while the
royalist deputies quarrelled, Louis-Napoleon, making full use of his
official position, never missed an opportunity to address their electors, the notables, large landowners, bankers, and industrial magnates. These gentlemen were not blinded by royalist superstitions.

To them what really mattered was not the color of the flag or the name of the future master, but the vigor with which this master, whoever he might be, would protect their interests. With each passing day, their conviction grew that Prince Louis was their man.

He used a variety of means to convince them. While he himself presented his case on rational grounds, less refined agents intimated that it would be dangerous for the conservatives to oppose his plans and to turn down his offer of a pact. Determined as he was to assume full powers, he would, if need be, enlist the support of the "red mob." If this were the case, it would be impossible for him to follow policies favorable to the propertied classes. He merely wanted to help them, and they would never have to regret their rallying to his cause. However, should they decide otherwise . . . . Persigny excelled at this type of blackmail, and the results were excellent. At the same time, samples were shown of the methods Louis Bonaparte intended to use once the bourgeoisie had rallied behind him. His minister, General d'Hautpoul, established all over France a police network, the mere extension of which would suffice to assure once more the peace of mind of the respectable citizens. The Prince-President's most astute decision was his refusal to place himself at the head of a newly-formed Bonapartist party. He assumed the attitude of a man above party. He wanted to lead the whole nation, with the exception of those individuals who were neither French nor human, and whom he variously described as reds, anarchists, plunderers, or communists. In other words, he intended to exclude those republicans who were conscious of the social and economic corollaries of the term "Republic." This was the bogey he needed to perpetuate and increase the fears of the well-to-do. He was not above conjuring in his harangues a sure-fire, pulp-literature threat: the plot hatched by the "Secret Societies." The Family, Religion, and Property, all would be destroyed in 1852. There were, to be sure, a few secret societies surviving in the provinces. However, they had been infiltrated by secret agents and were totally incapable of any real revolutionary activity. But there was in Paris a powerful and active secret society, the ranks of which were swelled by military officers anxious to further their career: the gang of the Elysée. Louis Bonaparte, that old Carbonaro, was in his element.

As of December, 1851, neither the President nor the privileged classes were menaced by any threat of any kind. The royalists, who had lost their following, were utterly disconcerted. In Parliament, they represented little more than a nominal, divided, ineffective majority. At least three out of four among them had already secretly rallied to the Prince-President, and longed for him to overthrow the regime at the earliest opportunity. At the other end of the spectrum, the "reds" were in full retreat. They were without arms, and since they were harassed by a relentless police, they had neither the possibility, nor even the intention of mounting the least offensive. Louis-Napoleon decided to make his move at this time. His mandate was due to expire in six months, and, as the Assembly had already voted down a revision of the Constitution, he could not legally succeed himself. Though he might denounce to his heart's content the plots of the anarchists and the monarchists, the only conspiracies he really worried about were that of "his word of honor against his ambitions," as Victor Hugo put it; and that of Article 45 and the calendar, which combined to throw him out of office come next May. On the other hand, he urgently needed money. After granting him three millions in 1850, the Assembly had refused him the 1,800,000 francs he had begged for the current year. He owed a half-million to the Spanish Ambassador, and M. de Morny's private residence was about to be repossessed. It is easy to see that money had to be raised at all costs. Of course the easiest way to obtain funds was to gain complete control over the treasury. Finally, he knew that a coup de main no longer entailed the least risk. The Army and the police were well in hand, and the judiciary could be counted upon, as always, to pass sentence on any and all designated victims. Thanks to Montalembert and Veuillot, the Catholics were also behind him. Above all, he had the quasi-unanimous support of the men of property, who urged him to spare them the ordeal of the general elections of May, 1852, because all signs pointed to a strong upsurge of republicanism.

The President possessed a unique advantage over all the possible saviors whom the conservatives had considered in turn: the name of Bonaparte. That was the point which Veuillot gently sought to bring home to the readers of the *Univers*: "Unlike the names of Bourbon and Orleans, the name of Louis Bonaparte is not utterly and instinctively repulsive to the democrats. In fact, the monster [Veuillot's name for the masses] feels a kind of naive attraction toward the Prince-President." Indeed, the Prince himself, his past, and his illustrious ancestry appealed to the rank and file. His name alone was enough to seduce and quiet down "the monster." This was a most interesting development. The conservatives needed a strong man to cage the "wild beast" on the loose since February; to chain it once and for all to the grindstone. A subtle tamer to subdue the popular "tiger," and lead him, purring all the way, back into the cage, there to be safely locked up. Who could ask for anything more? Only Louis-Napoleon seemed capable of such a prodigious feat. The proletariat knew of his *Extinction du Paupérisme.* He had not been afraid to repeat in Rothschild's presence that "his true friends worked in factories and lived under thatched roofs." He was well liked in the working-class quarters, where his proletarian confederates spoke of the "socialist emperor." Of course he was ready to burn, shell, and destroy these same quarters in the event of resistance on December 2. But that was not necessary, after all, since they did not even stir. Did not the proclamation of the coup d'état announce that he had dissolved the Assembly because the royalists were about to restore the King, and that he had saved the Republic by striking first? The best proof was the abrogation of the voting qualifications enacted by the royalists, and the return to full and unrestricted universal manhood suffrage.

How ill-founded was the conservatives' terror of universal suffrage! Because it had let them down in 1849, they forgot that it had brought them salvation the year before. Veuillot might rail bitterly against the folly of an equalitarian franchise in the *Univers*: "I have been defeated by my servant, my porter, and my bootblack;" and Montalembert might become exasperated at the thought that his vote counted for no more than those of his valets and peasants. They forgot that careful use of this symbol of demagogic madness could easily transform it into a positive blessing. In April, 1848, the men of property, almost mad with fear and without alternatives, had known how to talk to the "monster." He had been cajoled; told that he was well-loved; that one had done him great injustice in the past because one had been unaware of his plight. But these days were gone forever; the time had come to make amends. The conservatives did not miss a trick: choked voices, pats on the back, promises, emotional appeals in the name of holy fraternity. Long live the Republic! The electoral manifestoes issued in 1848 by such stalwarts as Falloux, Montalembert, Persigny, Baroche, Thiers, Léon Faucher, which

Girardin hastily reprinted three years later in *La Presse,* were one long chorus of democratic proclamations. The cannons were not available as yet; the squads and the battalions were still being assembled. As long as one lacked in Paris the 60,000 needed soldiers, the only way out, when confronted by the horde of slaves demanding a living wage and the means to raise their children, was to use gentle persuasion and to put the mob to sleep with kind words. With its stupid candor, the mob fell for the trick. Miracle of miracles, it actually believed what it had been told! The masses kindly elected as their representatives in the Chamber the very men whose one thought had been to riddle them with gunshot. The blouses voted for the morning coats. The peasants chose their landlords as their deputies, and the workers their employers. The appeal to fraternity had carried the day. But it had succeeded too well ever to be used again. The masks had been removed in June. The wounded and bleeding beast had become wary.

A man named Bonaparte, uncompromised by the June Days, appealing to the masses, now entered the scene. The election of December, 1848, had shown that the proletarians looked upon him as a friend. Although he had done nothing to improve their lot during the three years of his Presidency, he had explained that he did not have a free hand, and that he was eager to do something for them. Their lot would greatly improve if and when he were granted full powers. Give him a free hand for ten years, and a new era would dawn for the workers and the Republic. The masses let themselves be duped a second time. The results were even more satisfactory than in 1848. At that time, the panicky conservatives had only sought a temporary expedient, a breathing spell until they were ready to open fire. They did so a few weeks later. Nevertheless liberty and the Republic continued to represent a threat. Today's triumph, however, was a masterpiece. Completely duped, the proletariat willingly and with the best of grace gave up the gains of February. It abdicated its powers and entrusted them to the Prince-President. It placed itself at his mercy. A master coup if there ever was one! As Marx was to write in 1852: "Universal suffrage appeared in France only long enough to write its own epitaph."

It is hard for us today to appreciate the relief and joy with which the ruling classes greeted the coup d'état. As the new, purging, regime, with its "army-like police and police-like army," charted its course, and suspects were being seized at dawn in the cities and the countryside, summarily sentenced, and deported to Guiana or Lambessa, the men of property were living in a state of euphoria. Cassagnac's reaction could not have been clearer: "We have just been liberated; that is the prevailing sentiment." Echoed Quentin-Bauchart: "The coup d'état ushered in an era of liberation." From all corners of France, the "men of order" joined in the applause. The men of order? Victor Hugo was to explain that their concept of "order" involved: "Perjury, plunder of the public treasure, courts-martial, confiscations, deportations, proscriptions, executions, massacres, treasons, the sovereignty of the sword, and ambushes."

"Respectable citizens can once again raise their heads, and the demagogues are shaking in their boots," Flahaut told his wife. "Praised be the man, who by 'his great deed' had turned the moderates' defeat into victory." This was the expression used by the Comte de Laubespin, Montalembert's cousin, in an enthusiastic letter to Morny. The abominable prosecution of the rich by the poor was at an end. The verdict was in; the question had been settled, judged, buried. Praising the Man of December 2nd, the Man of the Boulevards, in the December 8, 1851, issue of the *Univers,* Veuillot declared that "the threatened interests of society are now assured of protection." Cassagnac agreed that "the Prince would protect all vested interests." And the *Constitutionnel* announced on December 7: "It is now going to be not only possible, but easier to engage in big business transactions." It was the time of the locusts, and the backers of "strong governments" are noted for their big appetite. The antiparliamentarians had centered their attacks against the "Twenty-Five Francs"—their epithet for the deputies who earned such a scandalous salary for their services. Now in power, they rewarded themselves with emoluments which made the total payroll of the old Assembly seem rather paltry: 30,000 francs for Senators; 50,000 francs for M. de Maupas; 80,000 francs for M. Baroche; 100,000 francs for Ministers; 130,000 francs for Saint-Arnaud; and sixteen millions for the leader of the gang.

Happy days were here again! "Let no fears spoil our pleasure," gleefully proclaimed Veuillot. Thanks to the regime's henchmen all clouds had been dissipated at last. Freed from any and all restraints, the jobbers and purveyors could now expect profitable contracts from the government. "How wonderful, if one could believe that

Society will be safe for a long time to come," exclaimed Morny on December 5th. It certainly was. Less than a year later Proudhon justly remarked that: "Textiles, metallurgy, grains, spirits, sugar, silk, all industries and commodities are falling into the hands of monopolies." The banking world was literally living in paradise. As early as February, 1852, a decree authorized the creation of mortgage-banks —a field of unlimited prospects. Among the directors of the *Crédit Mobilier,* founded in December, appeared the names of the inevitable Morny, the Péreires, and Henri de Noailles. In his *Vie Ouvrière sous le Second Empire,* G. Duveau later noted that: "The number of magnates controlling the Bourse and the industrial life of the nation was becoming smaller and smaller. Even those among the well-to-do who were not invited to join the inner circle, and who were temporarily jailed for safety's sake, had no great cause to complain. With the utmost delicacy, the government released Cassagnac so that his marriage to Mademoiselle Odier, the daughter of a banking family, might proceed on schedule. Because of his own exalted social standing, Monsieur de La Gorce could never look upon Louis Bonaparte as a completely acceptable man. Moreover, the policies of the Empire often ran contrary to his interests. Yet, he himself could not refrain from concluding his book with an expression of gratitude: "Let us be frank and give credit where credit is due. The great service rendered by the coup d'état of December 2nd was to dispel for a time [unfortunately only "for a time"; M. de La Gorce was writing after the Commune] the great army of rebels and trouble-makers by an awe-inspiring repression. The coup d'état surprised, punished, and reduced to impotence the party of the never-do-well, undesirables, and failures. That was the real merit of December 2nd, and it is only fair to say so."

The "real France" could now enjoy itself in earnest. The "Imperial frolic," which Louis Bertrand was to call "a stopover on the road to anarchy," had begun. In the words of Marcel Boulanger, Morny's biographer: "Everyone expressed his relief and satisfaction by an unbelievable display of wealth." Louis Bonaparte held splendid hunts at Compiègne and Fontainebleau; and personally drove resplendent phaetons at high speed. Dashing uniforms and scintillating jewels adorned the balls he gave at the Tuileries. Every afternoon the matchless avenue leading to the Arc de Triomphe was crowded with elegant carriages. Coaches à la Deaumont, light coupés, miniature parasols, broad crinolines, the sound of supple harness and steel halters—all blended into a charming scene. Oh what delightful elegance! How good it was to be alive! How easy, how simple it was to carry on love affairs under the Second Empire! And what of that charming little Countess Walewska, the perfect hostess, whose guest list included representatives from the Court and the City, the Church and the Bourse! It was all true for a few, all too short years. As Louis Bertrand noted with nostalgia: "France then presented to the world the picture of a pleasant, brilliant, and happy life in a refined civilization." In translation, this meant that the haves amused themselves tremendously. But what of the masses? I once found in Victor Hugo's papers, quite by accident, an old newspaper in which he had underlined an article that had caught his attention. (The paper in question was the respectable *La Semaine Universelle,* a political, literary, and financial weekly appearing on Sundays. The issue bore the dateline, April 12, 1863). This enlightening article was devoted to the depressing topic of workers' housing. This was 1863, but the descriptions were such that it might as well have been 1848. The locale was the North, Roubaix, the caves of Lille. To be sure some employers had built houses for their workers. But most of them were without "windows," and the privies "were breeding grounds of infection." The "promiscuity" of life in the caves of Lille gave rise to the same old social problem: when asked by the judge who had made them pregnant, the girls did not know whether it was their father or their brothers. That was another aspect of the "Imperial frolic."

Social Economic Problems

Hendrik Nicolaas Boon

THE SOCIAL AND ECONOMIC POLICIES OF NAPOLEON III

Hendrik Nicolaas Boon (b. 1911), a career diplomat who has attained ambassadorial rank, studied modern history, economics, and constitutional law at the University of Leyden. This selection is reproduced from the published version of his doctoral dissertation. Although it dates back to 1936, this work still represents one of the most comprehensive studies of the social and economic policies of the Second Empire. The author gives a detailed account of the measures through which Napoleon III hoped to rally the proletariat to his regime. Boon, who is sympathetic to the aims of the Emperor, recognizes in the end that there was a wide gap between what he was willing to offer and the real aspirations of the workers.

The personal rule of Louis-Napoleon Bonaparte actually began on December 2, 1851. The advent of the Empire, a year later, was a nominal change which did not really alter the nature of his powers. The coup d'état thus marked the climax of the Prince's endeavors. The prize he had sought so earnestly was his at last. It was now up to him to show whether he was capable of bigger and better things than the preceding regimes. Above all, the time seemed at hand for him to reveal his own plans, and to give the country an inkling of the paths he intended to follow. Intelligent observers shared the opinion of the Austrian Ambassador, who remarked on the morrow of the coup d'état: "Louis-Napoleon is nearing the end of his journey. His knapsack is full of the projects elaborated during the long years in prison and exile."

His first task, however, was to consolidate his power. If the opposition in Paris was overcome in a few days, several Departments were slow to accept the fait accompli. It was necessary to resort to arbitrary methods: the workers' societies were either prose-

From Hendrik Nicolaas Boon, *Rêve et réalité dans l'oeuvre économique et sociale de Napoléon III* (The Hague, 1936). Reprinted by permission of Martinus Nijhoff. Editor's translation.

cuted or disbanded; the leaders of the opposition jailed or deported; and special commissions set up to purify the country from subversive elements. The personal rule of Louis-Napoleon was thus ushered in amidst repression and deportations. Doubtless, the President was not fully aware of the scope of the measures taken by his subordinates. As always the servants exceeded the orders of their master. When he learned of the extent of the persecutions, he tried to mitigate their impact by ordering a sharp reversal of policy. But the harm had already been done. Socialist workers and organizations had been the first, and often the only victims of a repression carried out by Conservatives. To them, the new regime bore the stamp of reaction, and the later benefits of the Empire never completely erased this first painful impression. Louis-Napoleon's partisans interpreted in their fashion the strong and popular authority which he hoped to establish. Even some of his closest friends, like de Persigny, had but little taste for the social inclinations and policies of the President.

His power once entrenched, and the spirit of rebellion crushed by repressive measures, the President felt secure enough to initiate his program of social appeasement and economic betterment. Was he up to this self-appointed task? An understanding of his own peculiar views can be gleaned from the study of his writings and early life. He believed in the promotion of individual enterprise through opportune assistance from above (a Napoleonic idea). He was an authoritarian democrat. All social and economic progress would emanate from the principle of authority, solidly established at the summit. A dynamic outlook and a program of public works would promote economic growth. Social improvements would be brought about through the enactment of legislation which the assemblies of the Republic had considered, but had not dared to impose on the country.

It is true that some of his projects were impracticable, and that he abandoned them on second thought. Others, reluctantly endorsed by his ministers, were either carried out half-heartedly, or merely became dead letters. For example, a survey on pauperism, which had been ordered by the Emperor, led to nothing. It was twice started, in 1856 and 1857. Statistics were collected, but the results were nil and the project was abandoned.

Napoleon depended upon his ministers and their staffs for the actual drafting of laws. To say the least, most of them did not share the Emperor's enthusiasm for social reform. Unfortunately, Louis-Napoleon lacked, in this as in many other areas, a precise, thorough knowledge of the question. The general outline of a reform program was clearly fixed in his mind, but the objections of the specialists all too often left him without a comeback. Moreover, he was held back by the fear that his initiatives might alienate the very people who had done the most to discredit the Republic and to bring him to power.

These restrictions upon his personal inclinations, however, did not become a real factor until a later date. In the beginning, strengthened as he was by the overwhelming popular endorsement of his assumption of power, he could govern as an absolute dictator. In the few months before the convocation of the new Legislative Body there was not even the semblance of a check upon his power. During this period, he engaged in feverish activity, and delighted in decreeing many things which the deputies had discussed in endless debates without ever coming to a decision. This was his chance to give concrete expression to the products of his hitherto frustrated imagination. He claimed freedom of action, and the work began in earnest. During his brief tenure as sole and absolute dictator, the Prince-President promulgated no less than eighty decrees. Along with repressive measures, were others designed to stimulate economic growth, and to reform social institutions.

Soon after the investiture of his new ministry, December 15, 1851, the Prince-President directed his Minister of the Interior to issue to the Prefects, a circular ordering a day of rest in all government agencies and enterprises on Sundays and recognized holidays. This circular was little more than an expression of good will on his part, for he did not dare enforce a compulsory day of rest in private enterprises.

During this first month of dictatorship, he issued another decree regulating cafés and taverns. This measure was inspired by what Louis-Napoleon had observed in England and in his own country. Over and beyond moral considerations, the decree revealed a barely veiled political purpose: "In view of the fact that the ever growing number of cafés, taverns, and wine shops is a cause of disorder and a source of vice," each Prefect was given quasi-absolute control over these establishments. They could not open without his authorization, and he was empowered to close them up "for the protection of morals, and to prevent public meetings." Since the habits of patrons of drinking establishments cannot be changed by fiat, this measure cannot be said to have reduced the number of cafés or curtailed drunkenness. Louis-Napoleon showed equal concern with the population's financial welfare. The government pawnshops were reorganized along lines designed to curb the people's need to resort to usurers. Many branches were opened in Paris.

A measure clearly revealing Louis-Napoleon's kind heart was the creation of "Chaplains of the Last Rites." Many among the poor of Paris had to be buried without the prayers of the Church because they did not have the means to pay for this ceremonial. At the expense of the state, special vicars with the title of "Chaplains of the Last Rites" were assigned to the Paris cemeteries. At the family's request, they would officiate at the funeral of deceased who would otherwise have been denied a religious burial. An intimate of Louis-Napoleon recalled at the time how the Prince had once reflected upon the obligations of society toward the poor and needy: "I often think of society's duty toward the disinherited, and the more I study the question, the more I become convinced that much remains to be done in this field. Should I someday be in a position to do something about it, I shall not fail to try to correct this wrong." He never forgot Napoleon I's dictum: "One has no right to deprive the poor, merely because they are poor, of the things that console them of their poverty."

The most important measure toward the realization of Louis-Napoleon's social ideas, during these months of dictatorship, was the confiscation of the better part of the estate of the Orleans family. It is not our purpose to pass judgment on the political consequences of this act. Let it merely be said that they were considerable, and that four ministers resigned immediately after the promulgation of the decree. The important thing is that, in an attempt to make up for the despoiling of a family which was still held in high esteem in many parts of the land, Louis-Napoleon allocated the revenue to projects of uncontested worth. Now, at last, he possessed the huge sums needed to carry out some of his favorite reforms. Each article of the decree was in effect a point in his program, and, of all the acts of this period, this was the one which most particularly bore his mark.

Ten millions of the expected income would go to credit unions; another ten millions would be spent on the improvement of workmen's dwellings in industrial centers; and yet another ten millions were set aside for the establishment of mortgage banks, subject to certain government regulations, in those Departments where they were most needed. Finally, five millions were allocated to the creation of a retirement fund for the poorer parish priests.

The spurring of credit unions, improvement of workmen's housing, and founding of retirement funds—all sum up and characterize the legislative achievements of the authoritarian regime. In addition, a number of decrees enacted by previous administrations (such as those dealing with boards of arbitration and workmen's certificates) were either revised or enforced. This just about completes the list of the principal social measures which can be credited, in varying degree, to the initiative of Louis-Napoleon Bonaparte during the first years of the Empire.

But is it possible to give the Emperor so much credit for the social achievements of his government? Napoleon's personal contribution is very difficult to assess. The formal, dry wording of the laws provides no clue as to the identity of their original sponsor. It is certain that he did not dominate the administration to the extent which his uncle once had. The will may have been there, but the capacity was lacking. Still, he was the master of his government, and there was no power in the land to prevent the carrying out of his policies. While he sought information and advice, the final decisions were his alone. In 1854, he told a visitor that he did not allow his ministers freely to discuss affairs of state. He himself fixed the agenda for the cabinet meetings which were held several times a week. He liked to have his ministers debate the pros and cons of a given measure. On such occasions he seldom intervened, but seemed content merely to listen. The final decision was taken in his study, in the presence of the minister concerned. Most of the social measures of his reign were decided within the walls of this small private study. The documents tell us very little about these final exchanges of ideas between the Emperor and his ministers. On occasion, a speaker in the Chamber, hoping to flatter his master, praised the leading role he had played in the formulation of a proposed measure. This often served as a reminder to the docile representatives that they should be careful in their criticism of a proposal which obviously meant much to the Sovereign. This was not a superfluous warning, since the highly conservative majority in the Chamber had little taste for the Emperor's reforms. Through his experience with the daily routine of a complex administrative machinery, Napoleon became aware of the inherent difficulties of governing. The practice of power soon taught him that it was one thing to dream about the regeneration of society along the peaceful shores of Lake Constance, and quite another actually to reform a large country like France.

. . . Although the workers' movement had been smothered by the repression which followed the coup d'état, it retained more vitality than first meets the eye. The natural course of economic development, the increasing use and importance of machinery, and the consolidation of large-scale industrial enterprises tended to standardize the conditions of workers in all countries. Easier and more rapid modes of communications further served to minimize local differences in labor conditions. In the large urban centers, the workers were becoming conscious of the strength of their numbers. The birth of a great proletarian movement seemed imminent.

The Empire could not hope to repress this ever-growing multitude in the long run. Napoleon III, who was well aware of the fact, tried to lead and channel the movement before it ran out of control. His fundamental aim was to satisfy the legitimate material and social demands of the workers, thus rallying them to the Empire and turning their minds away from politics. Moreover, it would be much simpler for him to carry out the desired social reforms with the overt support of the working class, than to try to push them through a reluctant bureaucracy. Since the imperial police had thus far systematically crushed any and all attempts of the workers to organize, a means had to be devised for them to express their wants. The Emperor could not possibly enter into direct contact with their leaders without giving away his hand.

He finally decided to approach the workers through his cousin, Prince Napoleon. The latter understood the Emperor's social goals and did his best to help him. Their friendship dated back to the days at Arenenberg, where Louis-Napoleon had enjoyed explaining his program to his younger cousin. Although Prince Napoleon often embarrassed the Emperor through his thoughtless speeches and unjustifiable criticisms, the two men were in complete agreement when it came to the social question. This agreement is corroborated by their extensive correspondence. Let it be said, in passing, that this same correspondence also reveals a profound divergence of political

views. In any event, Prince Napoleon, who had widespread connec-
tions in opposition circles, sought to establish contact with the
workers. A journalist, Armand Levy, was his intermediary. A few
newspapers began suggesting to the workers that they should demand from the Emperor an amelioration of their lot. It was implied
that these requests would receive a sympathetic hearing.

The position of the faction which slowly gathered around Prince
Napoleon, the so-called "Palais-Royal Group," was thoroughly exposed in a series of thin, orange-covered, low cost "workers' brochures," which were widely sold in workshops. The Prince may have
defrayed some of the distribution costs, but the brochures were most
probably written by the workers themselves. The frankness and
daring of their demands is striking. Since all publications were subject to a tight censorship at the time, this in itself is the best proof
that the brochures appeared with the approval of the government.
The workers' demands were still diversified: some wanted the creation of syndicates, others a revival of the old corporations. One
and all proclaimed the Emperor's readiness to grant their wishes:
"We declare that the government will make good the pledge of the
Prisoner of Ham, and that the workers will be allowed to organize."
The workers sought to show that they had reached maturity. They
addressed Louis-Napoleon with no little boldness: "We firmly hope
that you will at last permit the formation of those delegations which
you mentioned in the most popular of your books, in order that the
People might daily express their needs and wishes to Your Majesty."

The idea of workers' delegations was picked up by the government, albeit not in the form desired by the authors of the brochures.
In September, 1861, the Emperor received a request that a number
of workers be encouraged to visit the expositions of Florence and
London. This request was endorsed by the Palais-Royal Group. There
was nothing new in the idea of sending a delegation of workers to a
universal exposition. But, heretofore, they had always been sent by
their employers. This time it was suggested that the workers should
select their own representatives. It is impossible to say who first
proposed this innovation. The idea had been in the air for some
time. One thing is certain, the Emperor immediately grasped its
significance. Prince Napoleon, who was chairman of the imperial
committee on expositions, was given the task of organizing the
election. The Prefect of Police tried to prevent the workers' elec-

tionary meetings on the grounds that they constituted a possible threat to peace and order. It took a direct order from the Emperor to overcome his opposition. Napoleon III had shown his hand for the first time.

The troubles anticipated by the authorities did not materialize. The Emperor insisted that the elections be held in complete freedom, and the workers proved worthy of his faith in them. More than two hundred delegates eventually crossed the Channel. What they saw in London incited both their envy and admiration. Upon their return, they demanded in their reports the liberties enjoyed by their English brethren. It has been said that these demands exceeded the wishes of the government, whose sole intent had been to give them an opportunity to study the methods of foreign industry. As if the government could have been naive enough to think that it could send workers abroad without giving rise to demands on their part. In fact, the Emperor's secret aim had been precisely to find out what the workers wanted. He would then be in a better position to ascertain to what extent he might possibly satisfy their aspirations. At first, Napoleon III had good reason to be satisfied. The reports did not reflect the spirit of class struggle which was later to prove so harmful to the Empire. On the contrary, the reports revealed the well-nigh unanimous desire to ease industrial tension and to promote the natural solidarity of labor and management.

An unexpected by-product of the workers' delegations was the birth of an international association of workingmen. It is beyond question that the formation of the International was a direct result of the contacts established between French and English workers at the London Exposition. The origins of this formidable force in contemporary history can thus indirectly be traced to the initiative of Napoleon III. Although it took him by surprise, the Emperor welcomed the advent of the International. Napoleon III, whose own plans for a European congress had just been defeated, had a special fondness for schemes of an international nature. One of the lofty dreams of his youth had been the organization of the masses: "Unorganized, the masses are nothing; disciplined, they are everything. As long as they remain unorganized they can neither speak nor make themselves heard; they cannot move or be moved in common directions." Many workers dismissed the organizers of the International as the agents of the Empire. The accusation was unjustified, for Napoleon never did more than tolerate an organization which did not seem headed for a very bright future.

The next measures initiated by the Emperor were indicative of the line he intended to follow. Napoleon hoped to win over the working class with a few laws designed to satisfy the wishes expressed by the delegates upon their return from the London Exposition. A new law on associations (*coalitions*) was especially needed, since the Emperor had all but abrogated the existing legislation by annulling those clauses which called for the punishment of strikers.

The administration did not really understand what the Emperor had in mind. Although the first draft of the law prepared by the Council of State did grant the workers the right to organize, it contained so many restrictions as to make this right illusory. The Emperor's advisors had taken the heart out of the bill. In this form, the bill was a disappointment to all those who had hoped for serious reforms. A conversation between Napoleon III and an opposition deputy showed that this first draft was not at all to his liking. The sovereign was indignant when he learned that the intended bill did nothing to better the lot of the workers. He expressly declared his intention to grant the workers real freedoms, and avowed that he would not be satisfied with half-measures. In order that his views might prevail, he assigned the task of drafting a new bill to Ollivier, a member of the opposition. Ollivier's later boast that he had first suggested the law to the Emperor was a twisting of the facts. He merely wrote a new version of the Council of State's project, in which the word "association" did not appear. The Chambers, bowing before the Sovereign's will, passed the bill with more resignation than enthusiasm.

The fact that the bill had been drafted by a member of the opposition was unfortunate, for many observers came to the conclusion that Napoleon III had been forced to make a concession which it was no longer in his power to refuse. Of course, this was the reverse of the truth. In the words of one of the Emperor's intimates: "It is imperative that posterity should know that the bill was not imposed on the Emperor, but that he approved of any and all measures which might extend civil liberties without endangering order or compromising the future." Just the same, Napoleon III's failure to give explicit direction to the Council of State from the start is to be deplored. Moreover, even in its final form, the law fell far short of the workers' expectations. If they were given the right to strike, they were still denied the right of assembly. In other words, the law permitted them to act in concert sporadically, but it still withheld the right to form permanent workmen's associations. Much also depended on the spirit in which the law was to be applied.

Now that the Sovereign had set his course, he should have continued on the path toward greater liberalism. There were indications, however, that his entourage was reluctant to give further satisfaction to the demands of the workers. Prince Napoleon tried to prod the Emperor to greater activity: "Good laws on the freedom of the press and the right of assembly, enacted immediately on your initiative, would be looked upon as useful and glorious reforms, not as weakening concessions of the last resort." But Napoleon III did not wish to dismiss the men of the authoritarian regime, who were irrevocably opposed to liberal legislation. He told his cousin that he did not want to appoint "new men." They would not have shared in past achievements, and their advent would amount to a repudiation of the majority of the Legislative Body which had always shown the utmost devotion to the Emperor. His taking the initiative of new laws could not be construed as a repudiation of the past.

Indeed, it took all the weight of his personal influence to push through the two great measures of 1868. In order to spur the growth of benevolent organizations, the Emperor wished to give his people complete freedom of association. Freedom of assembly, a natural prerequisite, was granted for all meetings of a non-political nature. In spite of this restriction, the bill met with such opposition in the Legislative Body that the Emperor was forced to ask Rouher to exert the utmost pressure on the deputies. The law on the freedom of the press met with equal opposition. Its passage released a veritable flood of criticism against the Empire.

The social measures for the improvement of the lot of the working class were somewhat more successful. In this area, the Emperor's personal initiatives antedated the enactment of legislation. In 1862, the Empress had founded the Society of the Prince Imperial. The Society's purpose was to provide credit facilities for deserving workmen, to make capital available to honest artisans, and to give the lie to the old proverb that "one lends only to the rich." One of the Emperor's oldest and fondest dreams, the creation of a sort of "loan on word of honor" bank, was thus realized. He labored under the illusion that a good reputation could be used as negotiable collateral. In times of crisis, the Society of the Prince Imperial made loans to workers who wished to purchase tools, machinery, or raw materials. The capital was raised through subscriptions—the Sovereigns themselves contributing 100,000 francs. The workers showed considerable respect for the given word, and repayments were made promptly and regularly. In any event, loans were made only to those who could procure two solvent endorsers. The Society of the Prince Imperial was not the only institution of its type. Another example of the Emperor's concern was a gift of 60,000 francs to the credit union of the Lyon weavers.

Another type of endeavor was the promotion of the cooperative movement, which was making great strides at the time. The statutes on corporations and joint-stock companies were a major obstacle to the movement's continued development. Since the Emperor had promised to free industry from any restriction which might work to its disadvantage, the law was first revised when the Treaty of Commerce was ratified. This new version still placed many restrictions on the founding of new corporations. The Emperor fully realized the measure's weakness and ineffectiveness. In a speech marking the opening of the 1865 session of the Legislative Body, he declared that he was ready "to remove all the remaining obstacles to the creation of societies designed to improve the lot of the working class." He thus announced his support of the cooperative movement. After long and careful preparation, the law was finally enacted. With the exception of minor regulations, it eliminated all government restrictions on the founding of corporations and joint-stock companies. Impartial observers have deemed that this law was one of the crowning legislative achievements of the Second Empire.

The Emperor, however, was much more interested in the promotion of the cooperative movement than in the details of legislation, which he was all too prone to delegate to subordinates. To this end, he established an Imperial Fund for Cooperative Associations with a capital of one million, of which he himself subscribed 500,000 francs. The fund was to help existing associations. Unfortunately, it was not overly effective because it operated on strict business principles, and few of its intended beneficiaries could meet the credit requirement. On one occasion, Napoleon III made possible the founding of a cooperative of silk workers in Lyon, by an advance of 300,000 francs, allocated from the funds of the Society of the Prince Imperial. He always liked to get his copy of *L'Association,* one of the organs of the cooperative movement, fresh off the presses. Cooperatives were in vogue, and Napoleon III did no more than stimulate a movement advocated by the best minds of the era. In spite of some failures, the movement grew rapidly.

The Emperor was much less successful in his attempt to control the budding labor movement. The idea of a workers' International was not incompatible with his own views, and he had looked upon its founding with favor. Its leaders soon came to understand, however, that many workers objected to their apparent collusion with the Empire, and the International's hostility toward the regime gradually began to crystallize. At congresses abroad, the delegates grew more vehement in their attacks. Matters came to a head when the report of French delegates to a congress held at Geneva was suppressed in France. The government's attitude was revealed by the answer given to representatives of the International who had protested against this interdict. Rouher told them that the ban would be lifted on the condition that they insert a few words in praise of the Emperor who had done so much for the working class. The workers refused to comply, and repression began in earnest. The International was outlawed in France soon thereafter. While the workers' show of independence may be admired, their refusal to accept Napoleon III's proffered hand served to delay the fulfillment of their social aspirations for many years to come. The Third Republic's suspicion of the demands of the working class was often to be greater than that of the Second Empire.

Still, the attempts to devise a "napoleonic socialism" continued. The financier Huglemann founded the Society for the Extinction of Pauperism, with the avowed aim "of assuring the welfare of the masses by consolidating their alliance with the dynasty." The Society sought to form an alliance with the International, but its leaders were so boastful of the Emperor's patronage that all relations were soon severed.

When the attacks against him multiplied during the last, unfortunate years of the regime, Napoleon III sought to defend himself by reminding his opponents of the achievements of the Empire. While he had previously tried to influence public opinion by publishing newspaper articles anonymously, he now sought to review the main events of his reign in the form of a novel. An outline of this unfinished project was found among his papers at the Tuileries. It was to tell the story of one Monsieur Benoit, an honest grocer of the Rue de la Lune, who had left for America in 1847. His only contacts with the fatherland had been through refugees, who invariably told him of a prostrate France, debased and impoverished by despotism. Imagine his surprise when he returned home in 1868: railroads everywhere, the electric telegraph, Paris transformed! The treaties of commerce had resulted in a general lowering of prices. He also marvelled at the Emperor's social reforms: old age retirement funds, the Vincennes Asylum, freedom of association for the workers. The principal achievements of the imperial regime were thus enumerated in haphazard fashion. This curious, and somewhat childish literary attempt is symptomatic of the importance which Napoleon III attached to the social and economic accomplishments of his reign. The very fact that he felt obliged to underscore these accomplishments also shows the extent to which they had already been forgotten.

In general, it is fair to conclude that Napoleon III's attempts to reconcile the working class ended in complete failure. Strikes continued in spite of the fact that he had provided full employment. The relaxation of repressive laws had resulted only in the growth of an organization irrevocably hostile to the Empire. The workers constantly ignored the advances of the Emperor's intermediaries. The satisfaction of social and material wants simply was not enough. Napoleon III may have recognized the symptoms of a movement which was gaining momentum, not only in France but the world over; yet he never derived any profit from what he had tried to do for the working class.

But was this self-appointed task humanly possible? After a description of the material gains which all classes of the population enjoyed under Napoleon III, a socialist writer aptly remarked: "Could anyone really expect always to control, or to mold to his own advantage, such great forces of history as the aspirations of the various classes and the hopes of the nation? One fine day, in the midst of their spontaneous developments, these forces turned against the dynasty which sought to control them."

It has been widely believed that Napoleon III dreamed more than he reasoned, and that he was a dilettante who lacked determination. Yet the facts speak for themselves. How can anyone deny the will-power of a man to whom France owed the transformation of Paris, the Treaty of Commerce, and so much social legislation? It is undeniable that he was a dreamer. We have noted his enthusiasm for utopian and impracticable projects which amounted to little more than pious intentions. But there was also a practical bent to his mind; and, when he faced up to realities, he was capable of following paths, where a man less determined to do good might have feared to tread.

It is easy to say that nothing in Napoleon III's social and economic program was original, that he merely followed England's example, and that any other sovereign would have followed the same course, because it was prescribed by the nature of things. Such an interpretation brings to mind the detractors of Christopher Columbus, who argued that anybody else could have discovered the New World. Napoleon III had the courage to undertake what others had merely thought of doing. He was just as much of an innovator in the socio-economic sphere as Bismarck and Cavour were in politics. His were lasting accomplishments. The Republic may have repudiated his name, but it could not undo the social and economic work of the Second Empire.

Taine once said of Napoleon I that he was a genius who belonged to another age; that he was a XVth century *condottiere.* While Napoleon III may be obscured by the shadow of his great uncle, no one would deny that he was a man of his century. He was even ahead of his times in many respects, and he foresaw the need for new institutions which did not fully materialize until our own day and age.

We owe to a musician, Liszt, the flattering but profound observation which best sums up the social and economic accomplishments of Louis-Napoleon. The Emperor was complaining about the burdens of his office: "Some problems seem insoluble," he said, "there are days when I feel as old as a century." Replied Liszt: "You are the century."

David I. Kulstein

FRENCH WORKERS AND THE SECOND EMPIRE

David I. Kulstein (b. 1916) did his undergraduate work at Washington University, studied at the University of Paris, and earned a Ph.D. from Harvard. He has been a member of the History Department at San Jose State College since 1958. Professor Kulstein's research interests have centered on the social problems of nineteenth century France. Based on solid archival material, his evaluation of the attitude of French workers towards the Second Empire might well serve as a model of monographic literature.

Can any valid generalizations be made about the attitude of workers towards the Second Empire during the years 1852–1858? For one thing, little active worker opposition existed. Often the very reports that expressed alarm at the persistence of republican and socialist ideas among workers insisted upon the prevailing "calm" and "tranquility." Cases of overt opposition by workers were usually not very serious: seditious songs and shouts, the posting of anti-government placards, the distribution of illegal literature, the celebration of revolutionary anniversaries. On the other hand, it seems clear that workers, particularly in the larger towns, had not rallied to the Empire. They were generally cooler to the regime than the members of other classes.

Between about 1858 and 1863 the government was more popular among workers than at any other time during the Second Empire. Considerable opposition towards the regime still existed, and, as before, workers often voted for opposition candidates. The *procureurs généraux* still contrasted the loyalty of the peasants with the *frondeur* city workers. Despite these reservations, the official reports showed an optimism usually lacking in the early period, and even when workers remained hostile to the regime, some *procureurs* believed that with a greater effort by the government they could be won over.

There were several reasons for this more sympathetic attitude

From David I. Kulstein, "The Attitude of French Workers Towards the Second Empire," *French Historical Studies*, 2 (Spring 1962). Reprinted by permission of the author and the Society for French Historical Studies. Footnotes omitted.

towards the Second Empire. These were the most prosperous years of the regime. From all parts of France in report after report the *procureurs généraux* told of full employment and rising wages. Industry had perhaps never before been so prosperous in Alsace, wrote the *procureur général* at Colmar. The *procureur général* at Grenoble stated that factories in his jurisdiction were flooded with orders. And from Douai, a similar report of full employment and prosperity: "The working population has never enjoyed more favorable conditions."

Prosperity was not, however, the only reason for the change in the attitude of workers. They also approved the political reforms of the emerging Liberal Empire. And, equally important, Napoleon III's support of the cause of suppressed nationalities and his intervention in Italy impressed many workers, particularly the most politically conscious. The masses, wrote a contemporary journalist, admired Garibaldi and his red shirts "madly," and if they had had their way France "would have declared war on Russia in order to liberate Poland." As Napoleon III passed through the working class quarters of Paris on his way to the Italian front, workers cheered him wildly, unhitched the horses of his chariot, and pulled the vehicle to the train—an incident which horrified the republican and future Communard, Gustave Lefrançais: "The thing which occurred yesterday at the Bastille was truly odious." The *procureur général* at Lyons wrote that the enthusiasm of the working class for the Italian cause was affecting its attitude towards the government: "The Emperor was becoming its hero." Madame Cornu, an intimate friend of Napoleon III before the coup d'état, told an English enquirer that while the Italian war was unpopular among the upper classes, workers were crowding the recruiting office.

Signs of the new attitude were particularly noticeable in the Lyons area. In 1860 the Croix-Rousse welcomed the Emperor enthusiastically, a sign, wrote the *procureur général,* that "evil doctrines" no longer dominated this worker suburb. The following year he presented more tangible evidence of the changed worker attitude. Government candidates had gained impressive victories in local elections, even in the workers' suburbs, La Guillotière and the Croix-Rousse, "two arrondissements of Lyons formerly so wracked by revolutionary propaganda. We had hardly hoped for such results." An old Lyonnaise revolutionary, P. J. Benoist, also reluctantly observed that many workers no longer opposed the regime: "It is sad to say, but it is the truth."

The *procureur général* at Grenoble also believed that workers were drifting towards the Empire. "The socialists are losing ground every day," he wrote in 1859. And the following year he offered concrete evidence for his optimism: in municipal elections workers had voted for government candidates. In 1862 the Prefect of the Isère, which included the city of Grenoble, reported that workers in his department believed in the "solicitude of the government of the Emperor" for their interests. Later the same year the *procureur général* wrote that the working population of Grenoble, "which included not less than eight to ten thousand persons," did not even glance at the funeral procession of a deputy to the Constituent Assembly of 1848.

In the area surveyed by the *procureur général* at Colmar the attitude of workers towards the regime also became more favorable. In 1859 the *procureur* reported that workers had rarely shown more respect for public officials and their employers. The following year he wrote that there had never been fewer signs of unrest in his jurisdiction. A report in January 1863 said of the attitude of workers, "Excellent from every point of view."

Although convinced of the existence of a secret workers' organization that sought to overthrow the government, the *procureur général* at Douai, nevertheless, reported in 1862 that no previous regime had been so successful in gaining the confidence of the working class. His colleague at Orleans was restrained in his optimism, but he also believed that the opposition of workers was no longer as adamant as in the past; they were not, "as formerly, aroused by the reading of evil newspapers." The jurisdiction of the *procureur général* at Rouen was among the first to feel the effects of the cotton shortage resulting from the American Civil War. Nevertheless, he reported, the working masses retained their confidence in the good-will of the regime, "and as evidence of that confidence they have avoided to the present time any manifestation of a kind that might trouble the public peace." And a short time later he contrasted "the *frondeur* tendencies" of the upper classes with the loyalty of the lower classes, "workers, artisans, small merchants."

From about 1863 the evidence that industrial workers had turned against the regime was overwhelming: election results, official and unofficial observers, and from 1868, when it obtained more freedom and therefore became more representative of public opinion, the press.

The period opened with the 1863 elections to the *Corps législatif.* As a result of the continuing loyalty of rural France, the government retained a sizeable majority in the legislature. But everywhere the vote in the towns proved unfavorable; in almost all towns with a population of over 40,000, government candidates lost. Although Legitimists, Orleanists, and the liberal bourgeoisie also supported opposition candidates, the reports of the *procureurs* emphasized the part played by workers in the anti-government vote. Some officials now came to regard the working class as incorrigible, as lost to the government, and those officials who did not despair of the working class insisted that the Second Empire must do far more than in the past to win it over. Commenting upon the elections, the *procureur général* at Lyons stated that wherever one found workers, one found opposition to the government. The Commissaire of Police at Saint-Pierre de Vaïse echoed this view, "All those who live off their labor, all who belong to the working classes generally voted for the opposition."

Most of the other evidence from Lyons from 1863 on reveals the hostility of workers. In 1864 the *procureur général,* despairing over the attitude of workers, urged restrictions upon the right to vote reminiscent of the law of May 31, 1850 that disenfranchised many workers by a residence requirement. Occasionally during the last years of the Second Empire incidents occurred that briefly encouraged the public authorities at Lyons, but much more frequently the story was that of opposition, of defeats by government supported candidates in local elections. Accompanying an increase in opposition to the regime was an increase of worker class-consciousness. In 1866 the *procureur général* wrote concerning the attitude of the working class: "The worker should remain united to the worker, that is the only maxim they understand. Hatred of their masters or employers, that is their only principle of cohesion." In March 1870 a *Commissaire spécial* at Lyons reported that the idea had taken root among workers that their economic conditions would be ameliorated only with the end of the Empire.

The government had expected setbacks at Paris in the 1863 elections, but the extent of the opposition success came as a surprise. A pro-government newspaper denounced the ingratitude of the city for which the Second Empire had done so much. And it is clear that the newspaper referred particularly to workers. According to Émile Ollivier, the workers of Paris voted for Adolphe Thiers because the government opposed him. Throughout the remainder of the 1860's the attitude of the workers towards the regime remained unfavorable. As at Lyons, economic dissatisfaction was translated into political opposition. A police report in 1867 stated that workers, resentful of the high price of bread, had attacked the Emperor. In 1868 more liberal laws on public meetings made it possible for radical republican and socialist views, repressed since the coup d'état, to come out into the open. These meetings were very numerous, particularly at Paris. In 1869 a deputy to the *Corps législatif* drew the following lesson from the orators and audiences at the meetings: "The most undoubted outcome of public meetings has been to show that, since the Revolution of 1848, envy, hatred, and malice have made vast progress among the working class."

From every part of France from 1863 to the fall of the Second Empire, the reports of the *procureurs généraux* also revealed worker opposition to the regime. Occasionally a favorable incident, such as a victory by a government candidate in a workers' area, encouraged a *procureur* to believe that things were changing, but subsequent experience usually revealed that there was little reason for optimism. The *procureur général* at Rouen, for example, stated that the elections of 1863 marked the beginning of a change in the attitude of workers to the government.

Economic and social discontent, more than anything else, account for worker hostility towards the Second Empire during its last years. From late 1862 until the end of the American Civil War the cotton shortage created unemployment and widespread distress in the textile manufacturing regions, particularly in the Department of the Seine-Inférieure. In the town of Castres, in southern France, only 200 of the 2700 textile workers had employment in 1863. After the Civil War, the years from 1866 to the end of the Empire were marked by agricultural and industrial crises and a decline in real wages. From the legalization of strikes in 1864 to 1869 the government had tended to maintain a policy of nonintervention in labor conflicts, but in 1869 and 1870 it acted vigorously against strikers. As a result, workers came to feel that their employers and the government were united against them. On several occasions troops fired upon striking workers. In 1870 a great strike occurred at Le Creusot that tended to create class-consciousness among a category of workers that had hitherto shown little interest in political controversy—workers in large industry .

Another reason for worker discontent might be described by a phrase from our own day, "a revolution of rising expectations." From 1864 on, the government made a number of significant concessions to the working class, such as the legalizing of strikes and the repeal of an article in the Civil Code providing that in differences over wages the court must accept the word of the employer. The government tended, however, to grant these reforms reluctantly, to surround them with various safeguards, and, in general, to fall short of what workers asked. Thus, while it granted workers the right to strike, it refused to change the Associations' Laws, so that workers still could not organize trade unions. (True, the government frequently shut its eyes to violations of the law.) The economic historian Émile Levasseur, who began his career during the Second Empire, wrote that workers resented more deeply the ban upon unions than they appreciated the right to strike. Workers at Lyons, reported the *procureur général,* became more hostile and more demanding with every new concession. When the government liberalized the laws on the press and public meetings, workers at Lyons saw only the restrictions which remained.

During these years, however, when the attitude of workers towards the Second Empire ranged from legal opposition to revolutionary action to undermine it, a pro-Bonapartist worker movement emerged that sought to rally the working class to the regime. The movement began in the "good years," when the Second Empire seemed to be gaining in popularity among workers. The government, particularly the Prince Napoleon, the Emperor's cousin and leader of the Bonapartism of the left, lent a hand to leaders of the movement. Armand Lévy, a revolutionary of 1848 and an ardent believer in the cause of the oppressed nationalities, seems to have been the intermediary between the Prince Napoleon and Bonapartist-minded workers.

What is striking about the movement is that it attracted a number of intelligent, politically alert, and class-conscious workers, particularly the craftsmen and artisans of Paris, so often the backbone of revolutionary movements. A leader of the pro-Bonapartist workers was the typographical worker, Coutant, who before 1848 had edited a revolutionary journal. The shoe worker, Jacques Durand, a violent anti-clerical and a future member of the Commune, also was sympathetic with the movement and praised the Emperor for his enlightened views on the social problem. In the first years after its founding in 1864 some members of the French section of the International Workingman's Association (the First International) flirted with the Second Empire. Parisian members frequently read *L'Opinion Nationale,* a newspaper that supported the regime. French workers were, in fact, disturbed by the relationships between some members of the International and the government. When members of the International appeared in their places of employment dressed better than customarily, fellow workers would ask, ironically, whether the police had paid for the clothes.

The position of pro-Bonapartist workers was that even if the Second Empire had not yet done enough in behalf of the working class, it was a government above classes that did not rule in the interest of the bourgeoisie. The old parties, the fallen dynasties represented, on the other hand, special groups, the nobility, the bourgeoisie. And, as the typographical worker Bazin wrote, while these groups were concerned only with political reform, "the suffering people . . . seeks above all an amelioration of its condition and of its misery. . . ." And this had nothing to do with forms of its government; the Second Empire, because of its origins and its responsiveness to public opinion, was more likely to aid the working class than other regimes.

After the fall of the Second Empire some workers still gazed back longingly at the Imperial epoch. Albert Richard, leader of the First International at Lyons and an exile after the Commune, maintained that workers had more to gain from a Bonapartist Empire than from any other form of government, including a republic. At the death of Napoleon III a number of workers paid their respects, one carrying a wreath with the inscription, *"Souvenir et regrets des ouvriers de Paris à sa Majesté l'Empereur Napoléon."* In 1878 striking miners at Anzin raised the cry of *"Vive Napoléon IV,"* although other miners replied with *"Vive la République."*

Foreign Affairs

Nancy Nichols Barker
A HOUSE DIVIDED

A specialist in diplomatic questions, Nancy Nichols Barker (b. 1925) studied at Vassar and the University of Pennsylvania. She has been a member of the History Department at the University of Texas, Austin, since 1955. Professor Barker belongs to an elite group of American women historians who have made significant contributions to the historiography of France. Her inquiry into Empress Eugénie's role in the formulation of French foreign policy during the Second Empire is the product of prolonged and careful research.

A few days after the dethroned Empress landed in England in September, 1870, the British Foreign Secretary, Lord Granville, wrote: "I am glad the Queen thinks of writing to the Empress. Her misfortune is great, although it is much owing to herself—Mexico, Rome, war with Prussia." Bismarck, Bernhardi, and the Prussian historian Heinrich von Treitschke soon attributed the fall of the Empire to the miscarriage of an Ultramontane plot, inspired by the Empress and the priests in the Tuileries, to save the temporal power. Thiers went to London in the fall of 1870 and spread it about that Eugénie and the generals were responsible for the outbreak of the war. Prince Napoleon and Matilda were soon in full cry after the Empress as the perpetrator of the ruin of the Empire.

Many of these charges have little bearing in fact. But why did so many of the Empress' contemporaries hold her responsible for foreign policy? With no official function in the government except when Regent, how did she acquire such notoriety? Very recently, in discussing the work of Eugénie in bringing down the Ollivier Cabinet during the war, a judicious scholar has observed that the "special evil of despotism" lies in "the backstairs influence of courtiers and women." Yet no one has ever blamed the fall of the first Empire on

From Nancy Nichols Barker, *Distaff Diplomacy: The Empress Eugénie and the Foreign Policy of the Second Empire* (Austin, 1967). Reprinted by permission of University of Texas Press. Footnotes omitted.

Josephine or Marie Louise. What was the explanation for the Empress' special power in the Second Empire?

The personalities of husband and wife are one obvious answer. The sweet and gentle Josephine, all "gossamer and lace," bent to the will of the imperious Corsican. Eugénie, direct and outspoken, could strike *peur bleue* into the heart of the less resolute and more gentle nephew. Eugénie had certain decidedly masculine characteristics, although they did not destroy the femininity of her personality as a whole, just as the virile Emperor displayed certain qualities usually associated with women.

The relative ages of the couple and of their son bore significantly on the Empress' position. When she married, the Empress was a self-willed, poised woman within a few months of her twenty-seventh birthday—too old to be malleable material. But if Eugénie was no child, her husband was well into middle age. When the Prince Imperial was born the Emperor was approaching fifty and within ten years showed unmistakable signs of diminishing health and vigor. A regency was a probability if the dynasty was to be preserved. The Empress did not shrink from the responsibility. In 1859, Regent for the first time, she thought that he, not she, had bungled the negotiations for peace. In 1865 she was more than satisfied with her administration. On the return of Napoleon she confided to Metternich: "The ministers have not quarrelled, and I have kept them so well in hand that I almost regret being obliged to relinquish the reins. I will say to the emperor that I give him back a strong and united government, and I will beg him to take care not to relax the bridle too much." A year later she requested the Emperor to abdicate and confer the Regency permanently on her. Even in 1870, despite the vicious attacks of the press upon her and despite the disappointing reception she had encountered on her trip to Corsica, she did not fear to face the prospect of the Emperor's death. Counting on the support of the right-wing Bonapartists who had been thrust aside by the liberal empire, she planned a swift and forceful action to rally a new government around herself and her son. The general expectancy of a regency was not, in fact, foolish. When the Emperor died in January, 1873, the Prince Imperial was only sixteen years of age. Throughout, as the future Regent, the Empress was thus a political force to be reckoned with.

The Empress had no portfolio in the government and no constitu-

THE EAGLE IN LOVE.

FIGURE 4. In the mid-nineteenth century, sovereigns who married for love exposed themselves to ridicule. Although latter-day observers have viewed Eugénie in a somewhat more favorable light, the Emperor's choice for a bride was a mistake from all standpoints. (*Photo. Bibl. nat. Paris*)

tional right to entertain affairs of state except when Regent. But she possessed one matchless advantage over the Ministers. She could not be dismissed. From the time of her marriage she was, with the exception of short intervals, continuously by the side of the Emperor, where she could leave him in no doubt of her opinions and wishes. Napoleon could not even break temporarily with her and pack her off in disgrace on one of those long excursions to distant points of the globe to which he occasionally sentenced Prince Napoleon.

Napoleon I had divorced Josephine. But Eugénie's position as the mother of the heir to the throne was virtually unassailable. Napoleon III had not made a prisoner of the Pope, and he lived in dread of the censure of clerical opinion. In Catholic France, for better or for worse, at least officially, he could cleave only unto her.

The hybrid nature of the Empire lent peculiar strength to the Empress' influence. The national unity of France was not of a monolithic, totalitarian kind. Unresolved were the social and political conflicts inherited from the French Revolution. In the person of the Emperor the so-called two Frances—the republican, anticlerical France of the Left, and the royalist, Ultramontane France of the Right—had come together in a temporary and discordant union. As a dynastic ruler with the trappings of royalty he could not be republican; he could never be a Legitimist. No one was more aware than the Emperor of the shape of his problem. "People reproach me for having two policies," he once complained. "It's true—I am obliged to have two, for I can not be a reactionary in view of my origin and I can not be a revolutionary because of the dangers that would bring me."

Eugénie probably never understood the problem in abstract terms. In the early years she fluttered back and forth between such disparate heroes as the revolutionary Orsini and the Bourbon Duchess of Parma. Later she would readily abandon what seemed to be political principle because of an irritation of the moment. But usually she more or less identified herself with the conservatives. Realizing her influence with Napoleon they rallied eagerly to her. She and her "party" lent each other mutual strength. When Eugénie did not have behind her either the force of a large segment of public opinion or a strong faction of the Ministers she was usually powerless to accomplish much with the Emperor. With their aid she could remind him of the dual nature of his monarchy and draw him back from the revolutionary slopes whither he was inclined to wander. At first their efforts produced only minor but disconcerting deflections in the Emperor's course, as in 1860 and the spring of 1861; just as they seemed to have him secured, he would trickle through their fingers. Eventually they were able to effect a consequential reorientation of policy. From the security of her position as wife and Regent apparent, she could cross the master of France in a way no one else dared. Not even Prince Napoleon and the other members of the imperial family had the same immunity as she from public reprimand and humiliation. Thus, Ministers and diplomats could shelter behind her skirts and use her to press their views. Lack of synthesis was always the Emperor's greatest problem. Not only did the Empress not contribute to its solution, she was herself a major cause of his problem.

The perfunctory observer of the Second Empire, noting that its best days were before the Italian War, might erroneously see a causal relation between the entrance of the Empress into affairs of state and the beginning of the serious woes of Napoleon. She was Regent when he made what was probably the first really disastrous mistake of his reign—the premature withdrawal from the Italian War. After the war, because of his unfulfilled commitment, he was unable to begin with a clean slate. He was eternally apologetic to the Sardinians and permitted them unaccountable liberties. These in turn, together with the Venetian question, complicated his relations with Austria. Eugénie's record in the Italian War was lamentable. She had encouraged him to undertake it but then, by her alarms, contributed to his irresolute conduct of it. But hers was not the decisive voice which caused the Emperor to draw up short. About all she accomplished was a demonstration of her temper and lack of comprehension of political realities with her quixotic uproar over the Duchess of Parma.

In the years immediately following the war she applied increasing pressure on her husband and was able to influence policy more effectively than at any other time during the Empire. From a series of temporary triumphs, usually followed by a frustrating check, she progressed to the instigation of the Mexican expedition and finally to the capstone of her desires—the dismissal of Thouvenel. Mérimée was never more correct than when he predicted a dire future for his amiable hostess and for the Empire as a consequence of her handiwork in the ministerial crisis of 1862. Among other things, Thouvenel's disgrace meant that the Emperor had been persuaded to reverse his Italian policy of 1860 and 1861 and to participate in his wife's cult of the Bourbons. The decision was fatal. Austria, encouraged to believe she could at any time reckon on French support in wrecking the unity of the peninsula, deferred recognition of the Italian kingdom and refused to cede Venetia without concomitant restorations in central and southern Italy. Hence, in time, the Italian decision of 1866 to fight rather than to accept Venetia as a reward for her neutrality but at the price of her mutilation. Ironically, the secret French support of restoration redounded to the advantage of the Prussians, who caught the Austrians in a war on two fronts and were able to trounce them thoroughly.

The temporary ascendance of the Empress in foreign policy in 1863 brought incoherence rather than cohesion to foreign policy. She drove off recklessly in all directions. While offering the restorations in Italy as her pièce de résistance to Austria, she proposed to abet and exploit revolution in the Balkans and Poland. The Austrians were offered a conglomeration of terms so preposterously contradictory that they inevitably rejected them, despite their real desire to seize Silesia and contain Prussian aggrandizement in the north. In her conversations with Metternich on the proposed alliance she revealed her incapacity for diplomatic negotiation. Naïvely and spontaneously she babbled to the Austrian ambassador the details of the French design for the future of Germany, plans which above all else should have been withheld from him. The proposed division of Germany into two parts with Prussia ascendant in the north and the French advance to the Rhine were the very prospects which the Austrians had long combatted. These, combined with the other unpleasant (from the Austrian point of view) features of the schema, such as Austrian cession of Venetia and of her Polish provinces, aroused distrust and repugnance in the Austrian government. When Prince Napoleon had outlined a somewhat similar arrangement for French aggrandizement in a confidential memorandum, Napoleon had cautioned him "not to dance faster than the violins" lest the Austrians suspect his secret ambition. It is a pity that he was unable to keep his wife out of the ballroom.

If the French offer had been more prudently and reasonably stated, if it had not, as even the Empress vaguely sensed, enveloped principles of restoration in a cloud of "revolutionary perfume," Austria and France might have come together and largely changed the course of European history. During these negotiations, without realizing it, the Emperor approached the great divide between the successes of the past and the disasters of the future. The year 1863, not 1866, was the real watershed of the Empire from which subsequent troubles flowed. The Austrian rebuff of France and the consequent coldness amounting to hostility resulting from the abortive negotiations played into Bismarck's hands. Serene in the knowledge that the French Emperor would stand aside, he drew Austria into the Danish War and then turned against her to evict her from the Germanic Confederation and to form a Prussian colossus in the north.

Sadowa was only the inevitable, unavoidable consequence of the diplomatic muddle of 1863. It was nearly unthinkable then that France should break her promise of neutrality and bind herself to the "Austrian corpse" in its defeat. The French army, although capable of a show of force on the Rhine, was not prepared to sustain a major war. French forces were scattered in Algeria, Mexico, and Rome. The dilemma of the Empire was serious enough, yet still the Empress, hotheaded and impetuous, found a way to aggravate it. Before the Emperor knew the extent of Austrian losses at Sadowa and before he had thought the matter through, she talked him into a public pledge, boldly proclaimed on the front page of the *Moniteur,* to defend Austria's membership in the Germanic Confederation. When, upon reflection, the Emperor decided against a military demonstration and accepted the ejection of Austria from Germany, he had to humble himself and admit to the world his inability to carry through his purpose. The alteration in the balance of power by the creation of a great Prussia in northern Germany was in itself a heavy blow at France. But when it was coupled with the public humiliation of the ruler of France its effect was fatal. The public was as shocked at the Emperor's nonperformance as it had been jubilant at his earlier pronouncement of action. Perforce the Emperor was required to redeem himself before his people if his son was to succeed him on the throne. As Metternich later analyzed it, "Mexico was his Moscow, and Sadowa his Waterloo."

After 1866 it was merely a question of time until Germany completed its unification and brought the French Empire to its final test. For Eugénie the four years were a period of chafing inactivity in which she impatiently bided her time to wipe out the diplomatic defeat by war and save the dynasty. But it is useless to reproach the Empress, as did Ollivier, for resistance to Prussian aggrandizement. What power has ever voluntarily renounced its great position when it thought it had a fighting chance to retain it? But unfortunately, she hastened the day of their Armageddon. Both Emperor and Empress saw in the Hohenzollern candidacy an opportunity for retaliation against Bismarck. The Emperor would have been content to rest with the voluntary withdrawal of Leopold. Eugénie, spoiling for war and mistakenly confident of the invincibility of the army, supported the demand for the fullest satisfaction of French honor. Thus, France fell into the war, which might have been deferred, before the diplomatic or military preparations were complete.

By 1870 the Empire had metamorphosed beyond recognition. The days of its successful wars were long past; the authority of the Emperor asserted in the coup d'état had dissipated. The Empress was virtually a ghostly reminder on the political scene of the blasted hopes of the reactionaries. Excluded from intercourse between the Ministers of the January Cabinet and the Emperor, she kept to her palace haunted with memories of bygone triumphs. From there she fanned the revival of right-wing Bonapartism and the old war spirit which, in July 1870, flared up more brightly than ever before only to be snuffed out by the rain of enemy fire.

When the Emperor was a prisoner of the Prussians, Eugénie, in one of her flashing changes of mood, compassionated his distress with tenderness and affection. On the anniversary of their marriage she wrote:

> In happiness the bonds [of affection between us] relaxed. I thought them broken, but a day of storm has let me see their solidity and more than ever I am reminded of those words of the Gospel: a woman will follow her husband wherever he goes, in sickness and in health, for better and for worse, etc. You [Toi] and Louis are my life. . . . To be reunited at last is the end of my desires. Poor dear friend, may my devotion let you forget for one instant the ordeals which your noble soul has endured.

The letter is a moving one and does her great credit. With her generosity of spirit, her pluck, her perfect integrity, she was one of the most admirable women ever to grace a throne. In uprightness of character she was the undoubted equal of Victoria, whose life-long friend she remained. Even Prince Napoleon, in mellower moments, would concede the Empress a goodness of heart, although he would add that she was both passionate and ignorant. Certainly she was superior to the bewitching but irresponsible Josephine.

But her fine qualities did not add up to statesmanship. With regret, for her personality inspires respect and affection, it must be admitted that her influence very seriously undermined the foreign policy of the Empire. The record of her blunders is too long and involves questions of too great consequence for her role to be written off as one of minor nagging. On account of Mexico alone she must bear a large responsibility for the decline of the Empire in prestige and material force in its late years. In her attitudes toward Italy and Prussia she too often acted out of sentiment or out of the caprice of the moment and, many more times than the law of averages would ordain, tripped herself up with her own follies and repented of her own handiwork. Her reproaches shook the Emperor's confidence; her enthusiasms led him to commit some of his worst errors. He could neither depend upon her discretion nor rely upon her judgment. He could never expect her to be consistent. Chivalric and rash, she believed a noble aim and its realization were the same thing. Sober, objective reflection was beyond her. The harsh truth is that neither by temperament nor training was the Empress competent to make wise decisions on foreign policy.

Pierre Renouvin

NAPOLEON III, BISMARCK, AND CAVOUR

One-time Dean of the Faculté des Lettres et des Sciences *at the University of Paris, President of the* Fondation Nationale des Sciences Politiques, *Pierre Renouvin (b. 1893), has had a distinguished career as a teacher, administrator, and scholar. He is recognized as one of the leading contemporary diplomatic historians. Renouvin served as the general editor and himself wrote four volumes of the* Histoire des Relations Internationales *from which the following selection is taken. This work has been widely acclaimed as a fine example of modern French scholarship. While Renouvin gives due justice to the statesmanlike qualities of Napoleon III, he nevertheless concludes that the Emperor was no match for the likes of Bismarck and Cavour.*

Would the will power, the clearsightedness of a Cavour or a Bismarck have prevailed in the end, had not the new orientation of French foreign policy facilitated the realization of their goals? The re-emergence of France as a disruptive force was the one most important factor in international relations. This phenomenon cannot be explained in terms of the pressure of economic interests, or of currents of national feeling.

The pressure of economic interests? To be sure, the rapid growth of French industry led to a search for foreign markets. But to what extent would the upsetting of the territorial status quo further that end? To obtain her share of the German market, France needed only to negotiate a treaty of commerce with the *Zollverein*. Thus the question of German unification had no direct bearing on the case. One can even argue that unification might prove a handicap to the reaching of an agreement, since a strengthened Germany would be in a better position to drive a hard bargain. French exporters were obviously interested in the Italian market. Might not support of the Italian national cause be rewarded by an advantageous commercial treaty? While French business circles may have entertained such hopes, the present state of historical research does not permit us to conclude that this was actually the case. On the other hand, it is certain that French railroad builders were interested in obtaining foreign concessions. Here was a likely motive for French intervention

From Pierre Renouvin, *Histoire des Relations Internationales*, Vol. V (Paris, 1954). Reprinted by permission of Librairie Hachette. Editor's translation.

in Italy. Yet the conclusion is inescapable that the business world was always lukewarm, and sometimes openly opposed to the grandiose schemes of the imperial regime. If, in the case of the Mexican venture, the initiatives of Morny were supported by the Péreires, the Rothschilds were opposed to the War of Italian Independence; and, in 1863, the representatives of big business unanimously spoke out against intervention in Poland. As Disraeli put it at the time: "Peace had been saved by the capitalists."

The pressure of national feelings? It is undeniable that a large segment of public opinion still wished to see France resume a dynamic foreign policy, and that it had deplored the "passivism" of Louis-Philippe. Although the political manifestation of this outlook did not extend much beyond the Left, the mass of the French population was not indifferent to endeavors likely to tickle the national pride. But did public opinion bring to bear overt pressure in favor of the revision of the treaties? In truth, there is no evidence to that effect.

The personal concepts of Napoleon III provide us with the only real explanation for the new orientation of French foreign policy.

The Emperor was endowed with certain intellectual gifts: a broad view of things, a fondness for ideas, and a rich, if eclectic rather than creative imagination. In matters of domestic policy he was a man of his times. He understood the importance of the emotional currents of public opinion. He was interested in the problems generated by economic growth, and hoped not only to initiate a program of "agricultural colonization," but also to assure "full employment" through the encouragement of capital investment in industry. Finally, he showed some concern for social problems. His approach to foreign policy was European, one might even say global. He never viewed developments abroad from a narrow, national point of view. He felt that a true statesman must be inspired by an ideal, and never fear to venture beyond the beaten path.

These attributes were complemented by strong powers of expression. He was an engaging conversationalist, and, on occasion, as Queen Victoria remarked, he could become "truly fascinating." Yet his intellectual equipment left something to be desired. He had little sense of realities, and his intelligence lacked the capacity to study problems in depth and to formulate precisely the means to their solution. His concepts were far-reaching, sometimes audacious; but they were tortuous, often subtle, always diffuse. The Emperor did not feel the need to think out his ideas, to bring them into sharp focus. Because he believed in "his mission" and because he was wont to equate his hypotheses with established truths, he always started out confidently when it came to translating his thoughts into action. Yet this confidence was soon replaced by doubt and hesitance. He had a tendency to let things drift, to prolong his meditations, to wait until unforeseen solutions might suggest themselves. In his make-up, imagination always surpassed will power and strength of character.

While he liked to be kept informed and to seek advice, he was not the type of man to follow consistently the lines of action suggested to him by his advisors or his entourage. In fact his method of governing was to pit his collaborators against each other. He was especially intent on retaining sole control of foreign policy, since, as he himself liked to say, the ultimate responsibility was his alone. For the most part, his foreign ministers did little more than carry out his policies. He did not even always keep them informed of his schemes. He often leaked out information to the press or sent releases to be inserted in the *Moniteur* without the courtesy of warning them in advance. He conducted negotiations with secret agents behind their back. As Walewski complained to the Emperor, in a letter dated August 22, 1859: "The ambassadors, who know that the back door is open to them, are going over my head. They deem it their duty to consult directly with the Emperor on all important matters. Even our diplomatic agents are not sure of doing the right thing when they follow my orders." Thus, in the strictest sense of the word, he intended to, and did indeed play his own game.

It is extremely difficult to unravel his basic views on international relations. The Emperor was secretive, and he never revealed his inner thoughts. Once master of France, he never again discussed his plans before witnesses, nor did he put them down in writing. No wonder then that his foreign policy should have been the object of the most varied appraisals—both by his contemporaries and later by historians. Any interpretation of this foreign policy must doubtless take into account the views he had expressed in his books and articles prior to his advent to power. But it is even more important to judge him by his actual deeds.

In 1839, almost ten years before he assumed responsibility for the conduct of public affairs, he presented a blueprint of his aspirations in the *Idées Napoléoniennes*. Evoking what he claimed to have been the policy of his uncle, he emphasized the "European mission of France," and proclaimed the need for a "general organization" of Europe. The means to the end of this "European association" was the fulfillment of national aspirations—thus removing the basic cause for the continent's troubles. France must assume the moral leadership of this revolution in international relations. How much importance can one attach to these professions of the pretender? The time and circumstances under which they were made give them a strong propaganda flavor. Between 1830 and 1840, the advocacy of a European organization was a favorite theme in Saint-Simonian, Mazzinian, and Anglo-Saxon pacifist circles. Louis-Napoleon may have been tempted to show that he was on the side and shared the ideals of the "reformers." At the same time, he may have tried to reassure Europe by implying that the eventual restoration of the Empire in France would take place under the banner of peace.

How faithful did the Emperor remain to the pretender's program? He retained two of its cardinal points: the need to revise the territorial settlements of 1815 through a major alteration of the political map of Europe, and the desire to base this remapping on the principle of nationalities. Yet he never allowed himself to become closely bound by this same principle; and, in fact, he violated it in many cases.

Along with these "idealistic" proclivities, personal ambition and the desire to consolidate his dynasty also played a part. In the words of Albert Sorel: "Because of his origins, Napoleon III was forced to keep France dazzled." The wish to react against the drab and "mediocre" foreign policy of Louis-Philippe, and the intent to show what a Napoleon meant to the greatness of Franch were always in the back of his mind. Was there a better way to flatter the national pride than to cast France in the role of the "moral leader" of Europe? Of course, he would also have to seek more tangible successes. France would gain direct benefits, in the form of "compensations," as a result of the territorial adjustments envisioned by the Emperor. In this manner, he hoped at once to satisfy public opinion and to serve the interests of the state.

International Congresses were to prove the means to the end of his goals for France and for Europe. At each decisive step in the evolution of his foreign policy he clung to the same idea. On November 21, 1863, he declared before the Senate: "I hope with all my heart that the day will come when all the great questions dividing peoples and governments can be settled peacefully before a European tribunal." In a speech delivered in 1867, he went so far as to allude to the desirability of a "United States of Europe." Yet, he gave the lie to these pacific grand designs by waging unnecessary wars in Crimea, Italy, and Mexico. Are we then to conclude that his declaration, "the Empire is peace (Bordeaux, 1852)," was nothing but a smoke screen, and that, hoping to take France's mind away from her lost liberty by successes abroad, he had decided to rely on force from the very start? Such a verdict is doubtless somewhat summary. One may be permitted to believe in the sincerity of his pronouncements, for he did not like war, and he was profoundly shaken by the sight of a battlefield. Moreover, he may have been aware that he lacked the strength of character and the capacity for decision-making necessary in a war leader. But the peace he wanted was not the peace of the status quo. In the final analysis, he resorted to war because he realized that he could not obtain through peaceful means the results which he deemed essential to the "honor" and "dignity" of France, and to the interests of his dynasty. How could he have failed to understand that any change in the status quo might be heavy in consequences for both France and Europe; or, to borrow a phrase from Thiers, that *grandeur* is a relative thing"? Nor can he have failed to grasp the full significance of Italian and German unification. But he actually believed that he could remain in full command of the situation. He was under the delusion that he could give partial satisfaction to national aspirations, and then turn them off before they actually became dangerous.

There was thus a flagrant contradiction between his aspirations and his deeds. Only on two points did he follow a sustained policy, at least for the greater part of his reign: the coddling of that same Great Britain which had defeated his uncle, and the break-up of the united front of the "conservative powers." For the rest, as one of the foreign diplomats who knew him best once remarked, "everything in his make-up and in his actions was a contradiction." There was a contradiction between his European outlook and his desire to satisfy the national pride; between the means he envisioned and those he eventually used; between the boldness of his thought and the timidity of his actions.

Foreign observers were prompt to take his measure. Wrote the Austrian Ambassador to Paris, Richard de Metternich, in 1860: "He sometimes shows the lucidity of a genius; at other times he seems blind to the most irrefutable arguments." An English diplomat remarked that he wanted "to direct everything," but that he was quite incapable of doing so "either through ignorance or indolence." Bismarck held that: "He has some fixed ideas, but he never knows where they will lead him. One might believe that he has thought them out, and that he is following a fixed course. But as he tries to carry them out, he suddenly bares the weakness of his foundations. He gives the impression of a man who suddenly wakes up at the throttle of a locomotive that has run out of control . . . . He is not dangerous, he merely does not know where he is going."

How then could the Emperor have been capable of keeping in check a Cavour or a Bismarck?

Albert Guérard

A FORERUNNER OF WOODROW WILSON

*Born and educated in France, Albert Guérard (1880–1959) had a long
and distinguished career in the United States. A prolific writer on a variety of
subjects, he was especially successful at explaining his native compatriots to his adopted countrymen. Guérard must be ranked among the
earliest, ablest, and most vehement champions of Louis-Napoleon in the
United States. His* Napoleon III, *published in 1943, represents a landmark
in the historiography of revisionism. In the excerpt below, the first of two
selections from this important work, Guérard presents Napoleon III as a true
"European," a champion of the principle of self-determination, and an
advocate of the "congress system."*

In March, 1854, on the eve of the Crimean War, Napoleon III said
in his address to the Legislative Body: "I have gone as far as honor
permitted me to go. . . . Europe knows that France is seeking no
aggrandizement. . . . The era of conquests is over, and cannot return; for it is not by extending her territorial boundaries that a
nation in our days can be honored and powerful; it is by placing
itself in the lead of generous ideas, by causing everywhere the rule
of law and justice to prevail."

These words, which have the same ring as the Atlantic Charter,
represent his earnest conviction and his hope. He was not, like
Alexander, Louis XIV, Frederick II, and Napoleon I, crazed with the
spirit of conquest. Yet the record offers a very different picture.
In eighteen years, the Empire waged three wars with major European
powers, and in addition, sent three important expeditions overseas.
The contrast between principles and performance is glaring.

But the key to this contradiction is not to be found in mere
cynicism, as in the case of Frederick II, who after completing his
refutation of Machiavelli, grabbed Silesia against his solemn pledge.
Napoleon III was committed to a democratic dogma, the doctrine
of nationalities. To him, it was the very condition of permanent
peace; but it was bound to disturb the status quo. This conception
was in his mind when he spoke of "taking the lead in generous

Reprinted by permission of the publishers from Albert Guérard, *Napoleon III,* Cambridge, Mass.: Harvard University Press, Copyright 1943 by the President and
Fellows of Harvard College; 1971 by Albert Joseph Guérard.

ideas" and "causing justice to prevail." *Quieta non movere* was to him not so imperious a command as *Fiat justicia.* The oppression of one people by another seemed to him an intolerable wrong. In this he was in full harmony with the romantic humanitarians of his time, with "Young Germany," with Mazzini's "Young Italy," with Michelet, with Proudhon. On the throne, and to the great scandal of his fellow sovereigns, he remained attached to the faith he had professed when he was a conspirator and a Utopian publicist. It is not for us to sneer: his ideal was essentially the same as Woodrow Wilson's principle of self-determination.

If he had been understood and supported, his aims could have been achieved through peaceful readjustments. For that policy was for him neither a vague dream like the Grand Design which Sully ascribed to Henry IV, nor a selfish plan to be imposed by force, like the "New Order" of Bismarck and Hitler. He had a definite method in view which would have been a substitute for war. His constant desire was to convene a European Congress which, like that of Vienna, would have reorganized the continent, but with *nationality* instead of legitimacy as its guiding thought. In this he was frustrated by the diplomats of the old school, too "realistic" to believe in anything but *sacro egoismo* and the balance of power. The only Congress that Napoleon III was able to hold, at Paris in 1856, was a tribute to his material prestige, but a defeat for his ideals: it achieved very little besides registering the paltry results of a senseless war. Thereafter, every suggestion for a Congress was rejected with ironical deference. Napoleon III was thwarted and derided, as Alexander of Russia had been, and as Woodrow Wilson was to be.

A Congress was intended merely to raise and define the questions to be solved; but no Congress of Powers had any right to take the decision out of the hands of the ultimate judge, the people. National existence and political regime, according to his doctrine, should have the same foundation—the consent of the governed. The will of the people, in both domains, should be ascertained in the most direct fashion, through a plebiscite. This method was applied when Nice and Savoy were annexed to France. Napoleon III secured an ambiguous pledge that it would be used in Slesvig; but the pledge was not redeemed—under compulsion—for another fifty-five years.

True to his humanitarian democracy, Napoleon III was not a "nationalist" in the narrower sense of the term, "Ourselves alone." A nationality for him was a family within the European community; he was first of all a good European. His economic conceptions went beyond the frontiers of the country he ruled. Instead of the snarling *autarkies* which were to torment Europe between the two World Wars, he was looking forward to freer trade; and he had to impose his liberalism upon the French business world. In curious harmony on many points with Henri de Saint-Simon, he had a Saint-Simonian faith in public works as factors of general prosperity; and he thought of them on an international scale. When he was a prisoner at Ham, he grew interested in the proposed Nicaragua Canal. The Suez Canal was one of his favorite projects, and he promoted it against the stubborn opposition of England. The one solid achievement of the Paris Congress in 1856 was to create the Danube Commission for the improvement of that great European river. He favored the first Alpine Tunnel, under Mont Cenis, between France and Italy. He attempted to establish a universal monetary union. He made a start in 1865, with the "Latin Union," which comprised France, Italy, Belgium, and Switzerland. In 1867, in connection with the International Exposition, he summoned a monetary conference; again, he had to encounter the full force of British conservatism. He happened to be fully three-quarters of a century ahead of the safe-and-sound. His support of Henri Dunant, the founder of the Red Cross, was not sentimental and platonic; it required vision and courage. We find it hard to imagine today what difficulties that admirable institution had to conquer. The military resented it; Marshal Randon, Minister of War, declared that Dunant's *Recollections of Solferino* was an attack on the honor of France. For conservative and "patriotic" officials everywhere, any international organization was anathema. The "gentle obstinacy" of Napoleon III again won the day. Cautiously but unswervingly he was striving for a new world order.

Fraternal nationalities without national jealousies, self-determined self-governing bodies within the European Commonwealth: such was the dream of 1838, and for three Bismarckian generations it seemed but the vainest of dreams. Conservative French historians, favorable on the whole to the home policies of Napoleon III, still condemn his "principle of nationalities" as a dangerous Utopia and the cause of all his disasters. Yet that ideal was revived with ap' parent success within the Soviet Union; and it remains our hope for the Europe of tomorrow.

Napoleon III expected irreconcilable opposition from those powers which were first of all "Empires" in the strict sense of that ambiguous term—loose masses of heterogeneous nationalities, held in subjection by a ruling race, a caste and a dynasty, Romanov, Habsburg, or Ottoman. In a democratic, scientific, industrial Europe, they were living fossils, impressive rather than formidable. They were weakened by their lack of organic unity, by their congenital sluggishness, by their paralyzing dread of modern thought. Already Greece had been emancipated; Napoleon III was most active in the creation of Rumania; the liberation of Italy, the resurrection of Poland, were part of the same program.

But the realization of this plan, with the strict minimum of violence, demanded the close cooperation of all the progressive forces —the forward-looking, liberal nations—and, for Napoleon III, these were England, Piedmont, and Prussia. This was the foundation of his foreign policy. He sought to preserve the Entente Cordiale at any cost; as late as 1870, he was still counting on the Italian alliance; and until 1866, at any rate, his constant desire was for a friendly and active understanding with Berlin. In all these hopes, he was disappointed; England was a dubious friend, Italy a broken reed, Prussia a constant and determined enemy. It was a tragedy for Europe that no one was found, in England and in Prussia, generous and far-sighted enough to understand and to support his aims. But we cannot lay the blame altogether on the selfishness of British and Prussian statesmen. There was enough ambiguity about the very nature of his regime, and about the temper of the French people, to justify every suspicion.

He knew England well; and, as a modern sovereign, he was deeply impressed with her economic development. He was aware that the Holy Alliance had never been popular in Britain, even among the staunchest conservatives; and he believed that, in continental affairs, England would always be found on the liberal side. So he deliberately sought England's friendship. To do so demanded boldness. There was no trace of Germanophobia at that time in France, but Anglophobia was rampant; and was he not the devoted heir of England's captive, the "martyr" of St. Helena? These prejudices he managed to conquer, in himself and in other Frenchmen.

He won over the fiery Palmerston, an old enemy of France, Queen Victoria, and even Prince Albert. But these were personal victories; under a tone of acidulous or ironic courtesy, the policy of the English government was consistently anti-French; and English public opinion spurned even that diplomatic veil. From the contemporary numbers of *Punch,* for instance, one might gather the impression that England and France were constantly on the eve of war. According to these cartoons—and to the solemn pages of Kinglake— Napoleon III entrapped England into the Crimean War simply to avenge a personal slight and to win respectability for his imperial swindle. John Bull did all the work, the French Frog claimed the glory. Because Napoleon III favored the union of the Danubian principalities, Moldavia and Wallachia, England opposed it. English opinion was overwhelmingly pro-Italian and anti-Austrian; yet as soon as Napoleon III intervened, English diplomacy sought to hamper him at every step. The Druses of Lebanon were massacring the Maronites; the Sultan was unwilling to stop these outrages, and France, as the mandatory of Europe, had to send an expeditionary force; but Lord John Russell treated the Emperor as though he, and not the Druses, were the arch-criminal. At the time of the Polish insurrection, England refused to cooperate with France in the defense of that martyred nation. We have already seen that in economic affairs, such as the proposed monetary union or the Suez Canal, England had but one guiding thought: whatever France advocated, right as it might seem, must infallibly be wrong.

This bickering policy resulted from a strange, but irresistible coalition of causes, some of them as ancient as the two countries themselves. There are now many orthodox Napoleon-worshippers in England, but in those days, the dread and horror inspired by the Corsican had not yet been fully exorcized. The Duke of Wellington, symbol of the great struggle, was still alive at the time of the coup d'état. If a nephew of Adolf Hitler should proclaim himself German Führer some forty years from now, our sympathies might not be wholehearted.

Then England was committed—and remained committed until 1939, alas!—to the balance-of-power fallacy. Whatever country appeared to dominate the continent had to be humbled, *debellare superbos,* so that England's rightful supremacy could not be challenged. It was constantly feared—and not without cause—that

France might seek to annex Belgium, and England believed that she could not afford to have a great power in possession of the Belgian coast. A curious delusion: from the strategic point of view, it was not Antwerp or Ostend that mattered, but Dunkirk and Calais; but in diplomacy, formulae are all the more potent for being hollow. The completion of the Cherbourg naval base, the expansion and striking technical progress of the French fleet caused natural misgivings in a country destined to rule the waves.

By the side of these stubborn and selfish prejudices, England's hostility to France had causes of a higher moral character. Liberty and Parliament were inseparable in English eyes, and the brutal fact was that, with the aid of the army, the President had dissolved the Assembly and destroyed the Constitution he had sworn to defend. Bagehot offered a less rudimentary interpretation of the coup d'état: but it was dismissed as paradox or casuistry. British society had little use for the Republican and socialist refugees, but the second of December was none the less considered a crime. To be sure, a military man, Oliver Cromwell by name, had also been guilty of a coup d'état; and Carlyle had recently (1845) turned him into a national hero. But Cromwell had one redeeming feature; like Frederick the Great, he was a Protestant. The French Empire was not merely tainted in its origin and loose in its morals, worst of all, it was Papistical. The lucubrations of the Reverend Michael Paget Baxter, *Louis Napoleon the Destined Monarch of the World,* were not a mere oddity. Many thousand copies of his horrific prophecies were sold; and what he dared to put into lurid apocalyptic terms many an earnest soul believed in a blurred but obstinate fashion. There was a baleful Satanic aura about the mysterious figure at the Tuileries, and his number was that of the beast.

Back of it all, there was the deep-seated aversion of nineteenth-century England for anything that savored of radicalism. The Second Empire, with its unconditional manhood suffrage, and its plebiscite, might be in theory and practice more democratic by far than Westminster was in those days; but it was not a "settled government," one under which "Freedom slowly broadens down from precedent to precedent." And the same objection held against its foreign policy. What Napoleon III offered might be in harmony with the desire of liberal Englishmen, but he proposed it in the name of a general idea, and it involved revolutionary changes. The ruling caste in England—

and it ruled almost without a challenge until the Second World War was well under way—kept true to the spirit that had deplored the victory of Navarino as an "untoward event": of course the end of Turkish misrule was devoutly to be wished; but only by gradual steps, and not for a few centuries. Napoleon III, on the contrary, an incurable adventurer, seemed to have no reverence for the wisdom of prejudice, the inevitability of gradualness, and the sanctity of vested interests.

The difficulties with Italy were simpler, but no less insuperable. Louis-Napoleon might be called an Italian patriot, even if he never was affiliated with the Carbonari. He had fought for Italian liberty in his youth; he never espoused with the same ardor the cause of other oppressed nationalities such as Hungary or Poland. Not that there was anything Italian in his character: ethnic types are delusive myths, but if we admitted their existence, Louis-Napoleon would have to be defined as a German rather than as a Latin. It simply happened that the Italian problem was to him an immediate reality, whereas the Polish and the Hungarian questions were but the corollaries of a principle. Napoleon I had, directly or through his lieutenants, ruled the whole peninsula; it was he who had created the magic term Kingdom of Italy; Hortense's brother, Eugène de Beauharnais, had been an excellent viceroy of that kingdom. Louis-Napoleon believed that he was destined to abolish the treaties of Vienna; and that meant, among other things, driving the Austrians out of Italy. Immediately after the coup d'état, he had publicly expressed his desire to help the Italian cause. At the Congress of Paris, he tried in vain to have the problem considered. Romantic or melodramatic episodes, the all-too-obvious wiles of Countess de Castiglione, the bombs thrown by Orsini, neither hastened nor deflected the Emperor's purpose. In 1859, after a secret agreement with Cavour, he had his way at last: he waged war on Austria for the liberation of Italy.

He entered Milan amid indescribable enthusiasm—one of the great moments in that strangely contrasted career. But the difficulties began immediately upon the lame armistice of Villafranca. He had rashly promised to free the country "as far as the Adriatic," and had had to stop far short of his goal; Venice remained in Austrian hands. Instead of unity, Italy was offered a loose scheme of federation under the presidency of the Pope. Napoleon's victories, we must remember, had been touch-and-go; the hardest part of his task, reducing the great quadrilateral of Austrian fortresses, remained ahead; Germany was arming on the Rhine. Italy's disappointment was unmeasured; in Turin, portraits of Orsini appeared in the shop windows.

The oddly assorted protagonists of Italy's liberation, Victor Emmanuel, Cavour, Garibaldi were sensible enough to recognize that Napoleon III had done his best, and that his intervention had been decisive. Minor difficulties were smoothed away. If Napoleon III ever had vague dreams of substituting his hegemony for that of Austria, by restoring the Murats in Naples and by making Prince Napoleon Grand Duke of Tuscany, this unspoken ambition remained the merest velleity. He secretly favored, while not only sanctioning at first, the union of Parma, Modena, Tuscany, Naples, and Romagna with the new kingdom. The annexation of Savoy to France was in agreement with the principle of nationality; that of Nice was more questionable; but both were confirmed by a plebiscite, and until Mussolini came to power, Italy never raised a serious protest against either. But the Roman question remained to poison the relations between the two countries.

Napoleon III had a clear view of the situation. He knew that the spiritual power of the Papacy was not linked with the possession of a minor Italian principality. He was persuaded that the independence and dignity of the Pontiff would be sufficiently safeguarded if he retained sovereignty over a Papal Rome on the right bank of the Tiber. This was the solution adopted in the Lateran treaties of 1929. But Pius IX rejected any compromise, and the French Catholics followed him unhesitatingly. The Emperor felt that he could not break with the conservatives who, so far, had been the mainstay of his regime. So long as the French troops remained in Rome, the Emperor was still "the Savior of Society," the bulwark against revolution. Napoleon III must have been sorely tempted to take his stand openly with his cousin Prince Napoleon. But we must never forget that he was a "democrat" in the full sense of the term. His mission was to carry out, not his personal views, but the will of the people; and he was persuaded that the majority would not support him in a conflict with the Church. From 1860 to 1870, he repeatedly tried to escape from the Roman trap. If he had preserved the mental and physical energy of his earlier years, he might have succeeded; one clear-cut sovereign will may go a long way to shape a nation's confused desires. But he was weary of strife; when he fell on the fourth of September, 1870, the puzzle had not been solved. The Italians, who denied their aid in his hour of distress, cannot be accused of ingratitude. After 1860, Napoleon III was no longer the generous ally who had defeated their Austrian oppressors; he was the foreign agent of international reaction who prevented them from entering their own capital.

In the case of Germany, the problem was considerably more tangled, and responsibilities even harder to assess. We repeat that in those days there was no Germanophobia in France, and, except among Prussians of the strictest observance, no deep Gallophobia in Germany. The liberals in both countries agreed in considering Prussia as the natural leader of a modern German nation. The French were still under the delusion which had made Frederick the Great popular in Paris; in the "enlightened despot," they chose to see the *philosophe* rather than the unscrupulous conqueror. From 1814 to 1848, Europe had groaned under the Metternich system; Austria was a reactionary dynasty, not a living people; so it was to the King of Prussia that the democratic Frankfurt Parliament offered the imperial crown. This faith in Prussia may seem to us naive: but we must remember that a whole decade later, the Prussian Diet, in the name of the modern spirit, was stubbornly opposing Bismarck.

Physically, intellectually, morally, Bismarck was the exact antithesis of Napoleon III. The two men met as friends; Bismarck's impressive bulk, his shrewd and caustic wit veiled in bluff heartiness, made him an oddity, but also a favorite at the Tuileries. But cooperate they could not: they lived in two different epochs. Napoleon III saw the essential aims of Bismarck, the unity and greatness of Germany, and did not disapprove of them; but Bismarck, more rudimentary, utterly failed to understand Napoleon. Hence his contempt for the French Emperor: "from afar, something; near at hand, nothing"; "a great misunderstood incapacity." They were the incarnations of two incompatible conceptions. Bismarck was a Romanticist; his loyalty to his liege and to him alone, his mystic belief in the sword, were frankly medieval. He belonged to the age of Wagner; in the industrial era, his dream of German glory was harking back to Barbarossa. Napoleon III had a realistic sense of the new world, the world which is still ours today. But the fossil had better cards than the forerunner, played a more unscrupulous game, and won the stakes to the applause of all good "realists." His triumph retarded by three-quarters of a century the normal evolution of Europe.

But it would not do to make Bismarck alone responsible for the conflict. There was much more to Germany, and even to Prussia, than mere Bismarckism; a nobler leader might have crystallized the confused mass of German aspirations in a totally different way. Still it cannot be denied that all the questionable elements we call Bismarckism were there, waiting only for leadership. On the other hand, Napoleon III and his people did not stand unequivocally for Michelet's ideal—all nations free and equal within a fraternal Europe. Powerful individualities in high places do make a difference; the surface of events, at any rate, would not have been the same if Bismarck and Napoleon III had not reached supreme command. Yet the misunderstanding between France and Germany was not created by them, and it is doubtful whether it could have been dispelled by them; for the only cure was to be found in cool analysis, and dispassionate analysts are never entrusted with power. The conflict resulted from historical confusions which, on both sides, blurred and distorted the nationalistic principle.

The Germans, divided into jealous petty sovereignties, were struggling toward some form of national unity, and in this they had the full sympathy of many French democrats, especially Napoleon III himself. But at the same time they were still haunted by the romantic ghost of the Holy Roman Empire. They could not make up their minds—they have not made up their minds even today—whether they desired to form a purely German family, among other national families, or to be the overlords of Central Europe. Thus the conception of German *Reich* was indefinitely extensible. It might mean every land where German culture prevailed; it might be all the countries where the Germans were a ruling minority; it might include the immense shadow of the old Empire; and even beyond those misty limits, it might reach for everything that the Reich would need to live, grow, and prosper. These Protean aspirations—a menace for all Europe—found their common symbol in the red, black, and gold of romantic Nationalism. Napoleon III's clear-cut doctrine of self-determination could not cope with this rich, organic, dynamic, and turbid diversity, which appealed at times to the will of the people, at times to history, at times to philosophy, and constantly to sentiment.

But Germany had no monopoly of "Metapolitics," if by that term

we understand learned and passionate nonsense. The incurable disease of Hungary and Poland, for instance, is that they are at the
same time present-day realities and dim gigantic memories; they
will not allow the Arpads and the Jagellons to sleep in their graves.
France—rational, realistic France—was not free from that blight;
and Napoleon III, good European as he was, with a valid and definite
principle to guide him, yet shared in the common delusion of his
people.

There also history was to blame—a history which claimed to be
immemorial, but was in fact very recent. At the time of the Revolution, the French had convinced themselves that the Rhine was their
"natural frontier." This boundary they had reached in 1795, and
kept until 1813. They lost it as the result of Napoleon's defeat; but
as late as 1870, they had never abandoned the hope that it should
be theirs again. They were sincere in their condemnation of "conquest." They did not seriously regret the precarious booty heaped
by the Grand Empire until 1812—the Illyrian Provinces, the Hanseatic
cities, vassal rules in Naples, Madrid, and Warsaw. But the left bank
of the Rhine was different; although they had held it for so brief a
period, they thought that it had always legitimately belonged to them,
and that in 1795 they had at last come into their own. The Roman-
ticists like Victor Hugo who were most friendly to Germany still insisted that France should recover "what God himself had given her."
The conflict flared up fiercely in 1840; mediocre but ardent war songs
by Becker and by Musset were hurled across the Rhine. Thiers, with
his defiant attitude, had rivaled one of Napoleon's achievements: he
had made Germany one at heart, united in the defense of the common fatherland.

The peace-at-any-price policy of Louis-Philippe and Guizot caused
a lull; but that policy, resented by the French, was one of the reasons
why the bourgeois monarchy fell in February, 1848. The election of
Louis-Napoleon proved, among other things, that France had never
accepted the *Diktat* of Vienna, ratified by a government of Quislings.
Louis-Napoleon's reassuring words at Bordeaux, "The Empire stands
for peace," were received with misgivings by the advanced elements.
"Does that mean," growled Proudhon, "that we are endorsing the
treaties of Vienna?" Note that peasant and bourgeois, in their secret
heart, wanted peace as much as Louis-Philippe ever did. But they
wanted a "peace with honor," in other words a tacit capitulation

under a blare of defiant bugle calls. So true it is that in every national spirit there is a blend of Don Quixote and Sancho Panza!

A similar ambiguity prevailed in the mind of Napoleon III. He was no firebrand. He believed in peace; he believed in democracy, or the consent of the governed, as the foundation of permanent peace. But he had made it part of his mission to avenge Waterloo and tear up the hated treaties. He could not bring himself openly to renounce the "natural frontiers" fallacy. So Europe, and particularly Belgium and Germany, were in constant dread of his aggressive ambition. The annexation of Nice and Savoy, harmless in itself, seemed the indication of an unswerving purpose. Today the Alps; tomorrow the Rhine. The "purpose" was a phantom; but a phantom can be most effective in creating a scare.

So far as Belgium was concerned, the "purpose" did exist, at least as a velleity, and there was some excuse for it. Belgium, subjected in turn to Spain, Austria, France, and Holland, had never been free until 1830; and at that time the liberal bourgeoisie, which seemed entitled to speak for the whole nation, had desired union with France. The veto of England, not the will of the people, had prevented the *Anschluss.* The Rhine provinces were a different affair. Napoleon III knew Germany too well to believe that Aix-la-Chapelle and Cologne wanted to become French. Had he followed his own principle, the problem would have ceased to exist. Yet, taunted by the opposition, he made half-hearted demands for "compensations," begging with feeble threats for what Bismarck bluntly called "tips." He thus accepted the two very worst guides in diplomacy, "balance of power" and "prestige." The result was one humiliation after another. Germany could not abandon even a few thousands of her sons in order to appease a saber-rattling neighbor and strengthen his rule at home. She knew that every concession, instead of satisfying France, would simply revive the impossible demand for the whole left bank of the Rhine. With every pretension, with every rebuff, irritation grew. If Napoleon III desperately needed prestige, so did Bismarck. In order to overcome local jealousies he had to show himself the uncompromising defender of the German heritage. Yet the worst peril, the Luxemburg affair, was safely overcome. In the early summer of 1870, it could be said that "there was not a cloud in the sky." We know how delusive was that apparent calm.

Napoleon III, the forerunner of Wilson, was in advance of French public opinion and centuries ahead of Bismarck. But his share of blame is heavy, for he equivocated with his own thought. The principle of nationalities, followed in simple honesty, would never have led to Sedan. But the heir of Napoleon the Great attempted to combine his peace ideal with the trappings of military glory. The pageantry of Empire did not seem an empty show; Europe resented it as a perpetual menace. The very brilliancy of the spectacle was a cause of weakness; not unreasonably, the opposition believed that the imperial army was exceedingly strong. So, as we shall see, Republicans and Liberals were at the same time urging a spirited foreign policy and refusing their support to the very measure which might have made that policy reasonably safe. Unfortunately, for fifteen years at least, Napoleon III as a military ruler bluffed Europe and France; it is certain that, long before the end, he was no longer bluffing himself, and that he did not fool Bismarck.

. . . We are not, this must be repeated at every step, offering a chronicle of events; we are seeking to understand Napoleon III. In such an evaluation, ultimate failure is an element which we have no right to disregard. Napoleon III did not meekly follow tradition, nor was he satisfied to live from hand-to-mouth; his distinction among rulers is that he anticipated and tried to shape the future; his genuine greatness is that, in many important fields, he proved a true prophet, and that the solutions for which he worked are still our hope today. By the same token, it must be counted heavily against him that in this case he guessed wrong, and that the thing he sought to create could not come to life.

But if failure must be admitted as an indictment, it need not be accepted as an all-embracing and conclusive condemnation. A man may fail, as Saint-Louis, Napoleon I, Lafayette, and Woodrow Wilson did fail, without being branded as a knave or a fool.

Lynn M. Case

A VOICE CRYING IN THE WILDERNESS

Lynn M. Case (b. 1903), Professor Emeritus of European History at the University of Pennsylvania, is another American revisionist. His own research on the influence of public opinion and the monographs of his many graduate students have left their mark on the historiography of the Second Empire. In the following selection Professor Case shows why the methods used by Napoleon III in his attempts to ascertain the moods and aspirations of his subjects might well "evoke the admiration of such moderns as George Gallup and Elmo Roper." He then goes on to give specific examples of the interplay between public opinion and policy-making decisions.

"There Was a Voice"

Public opinion was an important factor in the formulation of French foreign policy in the middle of the nineteenth century. Even considered from the point of view of the shackled press, one is nonetheless convinced of the influence opinion played. The very circumstances which show that the press was censored, bribed, bludgeoned, and inundated with syndicated articles all bespeak the concern over opinion and its expression. But on the positive side, the systematic efforts made by the government to ascertain genuine opinion beneath the sham of press opinion by ordering the continuous sounding of opinion by the procureurs general, prefects, and prefects of police are convincing proof that there was not only a voice but also loud-speakers by which the voice could be heard in accents clear.

The chancelleries and embassies, however much they might be peopled by haughty nobles and aristocrats of the old school, no longer scorned the voice of the people. Foreign ministers inquired, embassy officials watched with eagle eye, budgets provided for secret funds to bribe and cajole, and ambassadors reported on opinion unendingly in their roles as the eyes and ears of a distant sovereign. Election results were analyzed; the galleries were filled during legislative debates; stock-market quotations were scanned, not

From Lynn M. Case, *French Opinion on War and Diplomacy during the Second Empire* (Philadelphia, 1954). Reprinted by permission of the University of Pennsylvania Press.

so much in the interest of investments as for a barometric reading of the pressures of a certain class of the public.

Not only was great effort expended at the listening posts but also attention was turned to evoking expressions of opinion by trial balloons. Speeches were made, chance remarks uttered, articles written, documents presented, and pamphlets, especially, were published—all with the intent of eliciting responses. These devices were not in every instance to persuade the public, quite as often they were used as compasses to find directions or as registers to determine the amount and types of resistance to be overcome.

Among the various media by which opinion was given a chance to express itself, there were both poor ones and others more effective. The press was hopeless because of censorship, pressures, and bribery. There were rare occasions, such as the Danish War, when the press and general opinion seemed almost identical. But more often, as in the Eastern question, the Rouher speech, the anti-Prussian sentiment during the Polish insurrection, the mediation announcement of 4 July 1866, the newspapers were far from reflecting the public as analyzed by the more systematic procureur and prefect reports. Any resemblance between press opinion and public opinion was largely coincidental. The rigged elections and the packed legislatures were not even taken seriously by Napoleon III himself as weathervanes of opinion.

On the other hand, the intricate machinery set up by the procureurs general, the prefects, and the Paris prefect of police to ascertain and sample opinion, to check and countercheck it, to tally and analyze it, should evoke the admiration of such moderns as George Gallup and Elmo Roper. While it is regrettable that the reports of the prefect of police no longer exist, one must be thankful that the voluminous files of the procureur and prefect reports have given us ample and detailed evidence on the thinking of Frenchmen about their foreign affairs. A word should be said too for public demonstrations. Where they were spontaneous and not synthetic, they gave evidence of immediate and quick reactions to sudden events when the slower-moving administrative reports were not at hand. Besides, the parades, the cheering from the balconies, the illuminations, the bonfires, all not only registered reactions, they added a color and warmth so often missing in the drab reports of administrators.

"He That Hath Ears to Hear, Let Him Hear"

All of these arrangements for searching out opinion were not, like frequent administrative and military boondoggling, much ado about nothing. These reports, especially those of the procureurs general, were read, underscored, criticized, analyzed, summarized, and extracted. Rechecks on the surveys were made on critical occasions before both the Austro-Sardinian and Austro-Prussian Wars. If the reports had not been useful in more normal times, they would hardly have called for special reports in times of crises. Yet during the Austro-Sardinian War weekly reports were demanded of the procureurs general, and special reports were called for during the debate on the army bill and during the Spanish throne incident. At times the prefects were called in to Paris for direct reporting. The empress, La Valette, Cowley, Beyens, Rogier, Goltz, and Vautier all affirm the fact that the procureur and prefect reports were not only studied, but actually studied at the highest level of the emperor and empress themselves.

Nor was the attention given to these reports just to satisfy idle curiosity. There is ample evidence that the information was weighed in determining policy and in choosing the means to use toward certain policies. In at least twelve known instances involving important policy do we see public opinion influencing decisions: hastening the peace in 1856, delaying the Austro-Sardinian War, contributing to the sudden armistice at Villafranca, preventing the government from abandoning the pope's temporal power, pressing the government to return to Rome in 1867, compelling it to protest in favor of the insurgent Poles, insisting on territorial compensations in the direction of the Rhine, and rejecting an effective army bill. In two instances opinion stood out as the strongest influence in determining major decisions: in swaying the emperor against forceful intervention after Sadowa and in forcing the government to take a firm stand on the Spanish throne question and to declare war after the Ems dispatch.

Yet it must be admitted that public opinion did not always have its way. In 1859 the emperor went right ahead with his plans to precipitate a war with Austria, knowing full well that opinion was against it. Again between 1861 and 1866 the government undertook and persisted in the Mexican expedition over the strong and continuous protests of the great majority of the people.

One aspect of public opinion that must not be overlooked by students is its influence before the fact. The anticipation by policy-makers of what opinion would be is almost as important an opinion factor as opinion already expressed. After years of searching out opinion and studying its moods under certain circumstances the government was in a position to estimate the reactions of the immediate future. These calculations were just as valid opinion influences as the direct pressure from a developed opinion. It was quite a common occurrence for the empress to say that if such and such was done or not done, it would mean the end of the dynasty. The annexation of Savoy and Nice, the dismissal of Thouvenel and Drouyn de Lhuys, and the reoccupation of Rome in 1867 were all motivated by the anticipated effect it would have on opinion. The emperor's mediation announcement in the *Moniteur* of 5 July 1866 was clearly predicated on an anticipated expression of opinion. The expected result occurred instantaneously and precisely in the estimated direction. The only difficulty was its unexpected force. The sorcerer's apprentice had waved his wand, the waters gushed forth, but the poor apprentice was powerless to stem the tide. In the last months of the Second Empire, anticipated opinion played an ever greater role in the rapid events of the two weeks prior to the declaration of war against Prussia. Here fatal decisions had to be made before the cumbrous machinery of administrative reports could give accurate accounts of opinion. The government leaders knew that the Paris press did not speak clearly for the rest of the country. They had to judge largely by their knowledge of past opinion reports. The later Paris responses to their anticipations merely confirmed them and encouraged the leaders to continue an endless chain of further anticipations. Here we do not have a simple problem in cause and effect, it is a more devious one of the effect anticipating the cause on the basis of prior causes.

"Interest Speaks All Sorts of Tongues"

There is no doubt that the voice of the people spoke and received attention, but of more fundamental importance, what did it say? It was, of course, the noise of many waters, and not one clear call for all of France. Yet, in a few instances it seemed to speak as one voice. On the eve of every war except the last it spoke for peace; on some occasions when war was avoided, it had also called for peace, as in the Polish affair. On the question of preserving the pope's temporal power sentiment, while not unanimous, was preponderant for its preservation. Not just the clericals and legitimists, not just the wealthy bourgeoisie, concerned with temporal power as a property right, not just the peasant who somehow felt that its loss would be a sacrilege, but even the Protestants of Alsace stopped short of the ultimate in lawlessness and confiscation. Frenchmen of the Second Empire were not on the whole revolutionists, they were nationalists, that is, French patriots. When it became a question of French honor or French prestige, the voice spoke with little static. The proud ruler and his noble peers had no monopoly on sense of honor, for from the humblest cottage of the peasant to the smallest workshop of the city came renewed homage to the fair name of France whenever slight or insult was offered. And woe to him who would barter her honor for a mess of pottage! On these things there could be little doubt: peace, honor, and a modicum of reverence for their Holy Father.

However, beyond these few clear tones, the voice of the people spoke in many tongues. These divergencies may be seen better between classes than between political parties, because parties were either submerged or blurred during most of the regime. Of all classes the bourgeoisie and the peasants were the most influential. The bourgeoisie was by far the most insistent on peace, not primarily because war was thought wrong; the struggle for survival and let the best man win was the core of its laissez-faire or amoral philosophy. Rather war interrupted the normal calculations of business, it increased the taxes on the wealthy who would have to bear them, it decreased the credit of the governments whose bonds they held, it exalted the military whose power had more than once thwarted the power of the business classes. The bourgeois stand on peace came nearer to being one of peace-at-any-price than that of any other group or class in France. At this point honor and prestige took second place. Only under one circumstance do we see the bourgeoisie falter on peace: when the uncertainty of war or peace continued for so long as a deterrent to trade that they preferred war to the uncertainty.

However, France was predominantly agricultural. With the advent of universal suffrage the peasant's attitude was a basic consideration.

Here too was an advocate of peace. War or military service took his sons from the work of the farm. Invading troops had time and again ravaged his fields and blocked the outlets to his markets. Stolid and courageous, his was not a coward's heart, but the plowshare and the pruning hook were his weapons against a grudging Nature in his peaceful fields and vineyards. Nevertheless, the question of France's honor and prestige weighed more heavily on the countryman than on his bourgeois compatriot. In the rural community, reputation, personal dignity, and self-respect counted for much where one was known to all his neighbors. His soil, too, was the soil of France. Therefore he was as concerned over the good name of France as he was for his own good name. There were times when the peasant and his sons would fight rather than have France submit.

On the question of the papacy, Jacques the farmer was more realistic than he is usually given credit for. To him the religious hierarchy was mainly the local priest. The priest in prayer to him was natural, the priest in politics to him was ridiculous. For the pope to be priest and king did not suit his fancy enough to cause excitement. Thouvenel knew whereof he spoke when he said *"les vents ne sont plus aux croisades."* The peasant was delighted whenever the great landlords of France were forced to break up their estates; he had no qualms about seeing the pope bereft of most of his States of the Church. But when the Holy Father was reduced to a small plot of ground and to this remnant he held tenaciously as a small proprietor, this Jacques could understand. He supported this kind of temporal power as he would fight for his own landownership. Thus France as a whole never (Rouher's famous word) favored the disappearance of the last vestige of temporal power.

The city worker was almost an anomaly in French society. He existed in relatively small numbers in rather restricted areas of rare urban communities in a France which resisted industrialization right into the twentieth century. As a misfit he usually took the opposite side from that of other Frenchmen. In league with the lower bourgeoisie he could sometimes for short periods take over all of France from the central vantage point of urban Paris. He would proclaim republicanism, anticlericalism, chauvinistic nationalism, even socialism; but in the end the mills of provincial and rural Frenchmen, like those of the gods, would grind slowly, but exceedingly fine. Monarchy, the church, a more reasonable patriotism, law and order, and private property would be re-established for the long haul.

Less stable and economically miserable, the city proletariat was much more volatile. It sympathized with every revolutionary movement, be it republican, socialistic, or nationalistic. It fed on sensation and excitement. Hurrah for war! if it was to hurl itself against crowned tyrants or to liberate downtrodden peoples. Hurrah for war! if it would send France on a revolutionary crusade across Europe. It wanted war to vindicate the slightest reflection on France's good name. Here was the core of the war spirit in all the European wars of the Second Empire period. From the send-off they gave Napoleon III as he left for the battlefields of north Italy to the street demonstrations of those July days of 1870, the city workers were in the vanguard of the devotees of Mars. Hardly an armistice or a peace treaty received their wholehearted approval. But this voice was out of harmony with the big chorus of all France.

Likewise, in their extreme anticlericalism the city workers were an exception to the general rule. French attitudes toward religion and the church went from extreme Christian fanaticism to extreme atheism, with the vast majority in the middle, mingling skepticism with outward perfunctory religious observance. All the forces of clergy and lay clericals could not move the peasantry and bourgeoisie. Yet all the imprecations and fulminations against pope and popery, against power temporal and spiritual, against the very institutions of church and Christianity, hurled by the city workers and their petty bourgeois allies, did not swerve the majority of Frenchmen from their middle course any more than did the fanatical clericals.

All this the government learned and knew as it sifted the voluminous reports of twenty years of surveys of opinion. In most cases its policy in the Near East, in Italy, and in Germany did not depart too far from these basic attitudes of bourgeois and peasant.

"This Wilderness World"

However, there is a haunting feeling which grows as one studies the foreign policy of the Second Empire, a feeling that perhaps public opinion is a failure as an initiator or supporter of a proper and successful foreign policy. Looked at from the point of view of contemporary private moral standards the French people seemed to be right. They believed in peace, disarmament, the conference method, help for the underdog, law and order, justice. But when these ideas were insisted on by the people and followed by their leaders in foreign affairs, they seemed to lead to wars, humiliations, defeats, disaster, unresolvable dilemmas, and an ever-weakening position in the world. It led also to a serious disagreement between the people and their leader, who saw more clearly than they the type of world with which he had to deal.

Yet it would have been hard for the man in the street to comprehend the state system on the highest level of the world community; indeed it still is today, so different is the state system from the regime of law and order established within national boundaries. For on this highest level there was not one authority keeping law and order and dispensing an even-handed justice, but rather a multitude of separate sovereign-state authorities, each working selfishly against the others for its own national interests. Each state reserved for itself the right to observe or violate the accepted rules of good conduct—misnamed international law; each state decided for itself whether to make or break treaty contracts, how it would interpret rules and treaties, what alliances it would make and adhere to; each state decided if and when it would attack its neighbor for its own profit or survival.

And the principal considerations in all these international situations were not right and justice, but power and force. Population, resources, territory, armed might were the factors which counted on the chessboard of diplomacy. Not speeches and resolutions, said Bismarck, but blood and iron. There was but one god, Mars, and the threat of war, his prophet.

There was also the further complication in the nineteenth century, the coming of the industrial revolution. This gradually, almost imperceptibly, transformed the separate controlled national economies into one uncontrolled world economy. A civil war in far-off America crippled the French cotton industries for four long years. The factory women in the department of Aube who had had to turn to prostitution because of acute unemployment could not know that their lives had been changed and their morals undermined by a shot fired upon a place called Fort Sumter. And so the frantic sovereign states, becoming yet more frantic, dashed about for more markets and scarce raw materials, equipping their armies with the new ingenious machines and clashing with their industrial and commercial rivals in ever more desperate wars for survival.

The world community is then still a wilderness jungle; the state system is a system of international anarchy. There the moral code is turned about upon its apex; might makes right, and to the strong go the spoils.

How could the French people understand all this as they insisted on a foreign policy based on civilized principles? They were the heirs of the Roman law and makers of the Napoleonic Code. Their courts dispensed justice on the basis of right. Their contracts were enforced by a legal system. Their police, who kept law and order, were among the best in the world. Their economy was still much more agricultural and artisan than industrial. How could they, in their little nooks and corners of France, conceive that the world system was still back in the primeval forests of brute men? Of course, they had no such conception. They judged the world arena by their national arena. They applied civilized rules of conduct and high private moral standards to the untamed wilderness of world affairs. And thus they faltered and failed.

III THE NATURE OF
THE REGIME

Albert Guérard
CAESARIAN DEMOCRACY

In this second selection from Napoleon III, *Albert Guérard argues that the regime of the Second Empire was anything but a feeble caricature of the First. According to him, Louis-Napoleon, who understood well all the implications of popular sovereignty, made a bold and exciting attempt to adapt democratic principles and institutions to the conditions prevailing in mid-nineteenth century France.*

The first act of Republican France was to choose a Napoleon as President; the second was to elect Royalists as representatives; while the masses, in the great cities, were nursing hopes of a new revolution. Thus, there were three open conspiracies against the defenseless Republic; and Louis-Napoleon simply won the race.

More important, and less familiar, is the fact that *the French people had come to believe in democracy,* and would be satisfied with nothing less. The issue had first been clearly raised by Rousseau, nearly a hundred years before. It had been constantly debated in the course of several revolutions. The Romantic humanitarians such as Lamennais, Lamartine, Michelet, had for two decades preached "the sovereignty of the people." February 1848 seemed to have established that principle beyond dispute. But for direct democracy, which the people had been taught to expect, the politicians had deftly substituted "representative government," which may be a totally different thing.

Deftly: or perhaps unconsciously. It is easy, without Machiavellian pretense, to fall into such a confusion. Dr. G. W. Pierson notes that Tocqueville, an excellent observer and a cogent thinker, uses the word *démocratie* in four or five different meanings, without being aware that they are different. Under representative institutions, the electorate is a sovereign whose sole prerogative is to abdicate in favor of its delegates. It can pass upon men, but not upon laws. This is based upon the assumption that the masses have neither the means of information nor the competence to decide for themselves. It is expected that they will commit their interests to men of a better

Reprinted by permission of the publishers from Albert Guérard, *Napoleon III,* Cambridge, Mass.: Harvard University Press, Copyright 1943 by the President and Fellows of Harvard College; 1971 by Albert Joseph Guérard.

class, with ampler leisure, larger interests, a more thorough education. In the days before the railroads, the telegraph, the cheap newspapers, and widespread literacy, direct democracy was manifestly impracticable: even Rousseau believed that it could work only in small city states. Technical progress has removed these obstacles, and with them a cause of equivocation: if we do not believe in direct democracy now it can only be because we do not believe in democracy at all.

A difficult choice: America has never fully dared to face it. The President represents direct democracy; there is much direct democracy in the local governments, in the form of initiative, referendum, and recall; but the "representative" principle still prevails on Capitol Hill; we still shudder at the thought of direct democracy in national affairs. When President Wilson wanted a "solemn referendum" on the League of Nations, he could not secure it; the issue had to be tangled with a host of others in party elections, and the result was absolute confusion. The proposal to consult the people as a whole on the supreme question of war and peace is frowned upon by all sensible men. But the plebiscite that we so uncompromisingly reject in its honest form is surreptitiously introduced by non-constitutional means. A Congressman who is sternly averse to direct democracy will heed a deluge of mail from his constituents, a straw vote, or an informal poll.

Our own confusion may help us to understand the perplexity of the French law-givers in 1848. Their most glaring fault was that they had too much experience—in British Constitutionalism. They did not realize that "the miracle of England," as André Maurois calls it, is a miracle indeed, and cannot be transplanted. Rousseau himself, unrealistic as he is supposed to be, maintained that a country's institutions should be in harmony, not with an abstract pattern, but with its customs and traditions. Now, in their history of nearly two thousand years, the French had had thirty-nine years only of parliamentary rule, and they had just rejected it. Roughly, obscurely, the old monarchy had been the expression of the national will. The king, served by a body of experts, was the leader of the whole people, not the instrument of one party. The unanimous desire of the French in 1789 had been not to discard but to recover their king, who had been hidden from them by the courtiers at Versailles. The Bourbon dynasty, partly under the influence of a foreign queen, had proved untrue to its immemorial tradition; it had taken its stand against the people, and chosen to be at the head of the privileged orders. If it had to be removed, it was because it had allowed intermediate powers and special interests to entrench themselves, for their own benefit, between the nation as a whole and the sovereign. It was these powers that the people had struck down, and were ready to strike down again, if they should arise once more under new forms and new names, such as Plutocracy or Parliament.

We are not claiming that the peasants and workingmen of France had definitely evolved such a political theory, which is far from clear in their minds even today. But it was that unformulated doctrine—direct contact between sovereign and masses—that accounted for their obstinate loyalty to the Capetian dynasty, for their enthusiasm at the dawn of the Revolution, for their willingness to accept Napoleon's rule; under three radically different forms, what they sought was the abolition of privilege. They never attached any other meaning to the word "democracy."

All political parties, on the other hand, those of the Left as well as those of the Right, stood frankly or equivocally for a denial of direct democracy, for the privileges of some élite. The legitimists had insisted on divine right, sanctioning a social hierarchy; the Orleanists, on property qualifications; the Republicans, on a certain "Enlightenment," which meant the possession of the Republican faith. Thiers was, courageously, to attack universal suffrage as the rule of "the vile multitude"; and Victor Hugo, who thought of himself as the High Priest of the democratic ideal, had to draw a subtle distinction between "the People," whose voice is that of God Himself, and the mob, the abject "populace." The "People," of course, are the intelligent workers of Paris, who vote for the Radicals; the "populace" are the rural masses who, deliberately and stupidly, had chosen Louis-Napoleon.

If people and leaders alike lived in a cloud of ambiguities, there was one man whose thought on the subject was flawlessly clear, and that man was Louis-Napoleon. He had expressed his doctrine, not in chance remarks or in thunderous eloquence, but in a cogent little book, published as early as 1839, *Napoleonic Ideas*. This unequivocal manifesto had reached a vast public. Jules Simon might brand it as worthless, offering as irrefutable proof of its inanity the fact that he had never read it; but the masses had not been so supercilious.

Bonapartist propaganda was not merely vague appeal to the military prestige of the Emperor: it referred definitely to a system of government.

The outstanding merit of Louis-Napoleon is not to have proclaimed the dogma of absolute democracy; on this point, Lamartine was no less emphatic than he. It was, the dogma once admitted, to have faced the conditions that it implied, and this Lamartine never did. It will not suffice to cry lyrically *"Alea jacta est!* Let God and the people decide!" The more democratic the commonwealth is, the more urgently does it need order and leadership. Else the suppression of the privileged classes, with their traditional skills and their inherited responsibilities, would lead only to chaos. Democracy is revolution; it breaks down an ancient discipline, cumbrous and absurd in some respects, but, as a result of long adjustment, tolerably effective. To guard against anarchy, it must provide a discipline of its own. This discipline must seem rough and even rigorous at first, because it is unfamiliar; it will appear most obnoxious, naturally, to those who were the beneficiaries of the old system. The one justification for its rigor is that it be freely accepted; willing obedience is the reverse of servitude. When the new dispensation has been fully established, in the course of one generation, it will turn into a habit, and lose its stern rigidity. Freedom, in the sense of *ease,* will grow in the democratic world. But liberty is something to be achieved, not the initial step. In the terms of Louis-Napoleon himself, it must "crown the edifice."

At this point, we must remind the reader that we are seeking to understand the France of 1848, and not offering a solution for the problem of the "democracies" a hundred years later. Whether there was any permanent validity in Louis-Napoleon's system is a different question. The man and his cause have long been dead, and belong to history, not to current politics. What we are striving to establish is that France, in December, 1848, was not exclusively moved by a childish thirst for martial glory at second hand, or by an agony of reactionary fear. These elements did exist: but, deeper than either, there was a program, well-known of the electoral masses, and well-understood by them. It was that program which was freely endorsed by 5.4 million votes.

We have said that the thought of Louis-Napoleon was clear, so clear that it could be translated into the terms of a brief working constitution. That clearness will be challenged by the modern mind. We must remember that Louis-Napoleon lived and worked in the Romantic era. He freely used terms which, to realistic politicians of our own days, would seem absurdly mystic. For one thing, he thought of the Leader, who was to be the symbol of democratic discipline, as a "providential man," and he believed himself to be such an instrument of the Divine Purpose. This faith was ever with him; he finally stated it, in the Preface to his *History of Julius Caesar* (1865–1866), with an imperial brevity which makes Carlyle's eloquence in *Heroes and Hero-Worship* seem rather turgid. But he only expressed, in the language of the time, what the innumerable company of the safe-and-sane would name "legitimate ambition." A man proposes himself to the suffrage of his fellow citizens because he feels himself called to lead. Belief in his own mission is an indispensable characteristic of the apostle. Once more, we must attune ourselves to the Romantic key. Compared with the style of Mr. Stanley Baldwin or of President Coolidge, that of Louis-Napoleon's pamphlets is highflown; compared with that of Lamennais, Enfantin, Barrault, Pierre Leroux, Lamartine, Michelet, Quinet, Hugo, George Sand, it is singularly quiet and sensible. His faith in himself was "gently obstinate," not blatant; in spirit, in tone, as well as in appearance, he was the most unassuming, the least apocalyptic of political prophets.

We can translate Romantic Humanitarianism into terms of practical politics, and Louis-Napoleon himself did it efficiently; but a far worse cause of confusion was Napoleon-worship. He considered himself as the champion of a truth, but also as the heir of the Emperor, legally and in the spirit. This it was that had given him his start, both in his thought and in his political fortune. He was not moving on the same plane as other theorists of democracy: he was singled out by the faith and the prestige that went with his name. Yet we must remember that if in his mind "Napoleon" and "Democracy" were inseparable, Democracy was the permanent cause to be served, Napoleonism only the instrument. He never claimed power for himself by dynastic right, as a Napoleon; his name made him simply the defender of the people against selfish interests. In 1836, in 1840, he asserted that his sole aim was to give back to the nation her right to choose her own form of government. In 1848, he accepted the Republic. So we believe that he was sincere when he affirmed, in his halting speech before the Constituent Assembly, that he was a candidate, but not a pretender. Had Cavaignac or Lamartine been elected and *remained democrats,* it is at least conceivable that he would have served under them. The source of his power, this can never be sufficiently insisted upon, was the free election of the tenth of December. He could not cut loose from his Napoleonic origin, but his democratic ideal was prospective. His regime was not a feeble caricature of the First Empire, but something altogether different, and, in our opinion, of far more vital interest.

Alfred Cobban

A BOURGEOIS EMPIRE

A former Rockefeller Fellow for research in France, one-time Visiting Professor at the University of Chicago, Alfred Cobban (1901–1968) was one of the most active contemporary English historians. His duties as Professor of French History at University College, London, and as editor of History, *did not keep him from adding to an already impressive list of writings on a variety of subjects. This excerpt is taken from* A History of Modern France, *a study which incorporates Mr. Cobban's broad knowledge of the field. As the title of the selection itself indicates, the author considers the Second Empire to have been essentially a middle-class regime.*

A wave of economic expansion followed the establishment of the Empire. It was concentrated particularly on the development of railways. After a slow beginning, the companies were rationalized by being reduced to six, and the pace of construction was so accelerated that by 1859 France had nearly three times as great a length of line as in 1851. By 1870 France had almost as extensive a network of lines in operation as Germany or Great Britain. Railway development stimulated, of course, the production of coal and iron. The consumption of coal was trebled, and the use of horsepower in industry quintupled, between 1851 and 1870. The average price of steel was practically halved. The greatest of the iron-works, at Le Creusot, was

From Alfred Cobban, *A History of Modern France,* Vol. II (Harmondsworth, Middlesex, 1961). Reprinted by permission of Penguin Books Ltd.

bought by the Schneider brothers in 1836 when its annual production was 5,000 tons; in 1847 it was 18,000, and the increased pace of growth under the Second Empire is shown by the rise from 35,000 tons in 1855 to 133,000 in 1867. In the same period the foreign commerce of France practically trebled.

Meanwhile the growth of the French population had slackened, so that the increased wealth of the country was not swallowed up by the excess of mouths. Moreover the shift from the country to the town continued. The proportion of urban population grew from 24 per cent to 31 per cent, and this probably represented a rise in the average standard of life in the countryside, for it was the landless laborers and the poorest element there which declined most. The growth of railways, which played their part in facilitating the movement from the country, also broke down some of the traditional rural isolation.

The share of the state in providing the actual finance for this general economic development should not be exaggerated. Up to 1860 the public works program was financed mainly by private investment. Budgetary expenses for this purpose were indeed smaller than they had been under Louis-Philippe; whence those developments in which for one reason or another the private investor was not interested—roads, canals, ports—languished. The same was true of agriculture. The peasants, whose votes had established the Second Empire, were those who profited least from it. They were suspicious of all new methods; the legal structure of France protected the small proprietor in his jealous independence of any interference, and the sub-division of the land prohibited any general or coordinated schemes of improvement.

The program of public works which Louis-Napoleon inaugurated was in his mind a continuation of the policy of the First Empire. He himself wrote of Napoleon I, "The public works, which the Emperor put into operation on such a large scale, were not only one of the principal causes of domestic prosperity, they even promoted great social progress." While these motives were certainly present to the mind of Napoleon III, the propaganda value of public works was also not absent, particularly if they could be effected in full view of the public. The improvement of Paris, in continuation of the work of Napoleon I, was therefore among the first projects to be taken in hand after the coup d'état.

The need to render Paris, like all the other great urban agglomerations of Europe, habitable, was patent enough; but it would be a mistake to attribute the improvements solely to the pressure of hard facts. Great towns had always been unsanitary, stinking haunts of dirt and disease. In most of the world they were to remain such for generations later. Reforms, in Paris as in London, did not come about by the automatic pressure of circumstances; they were the conscious achievement of the disciples of a Saint-Simon and a Bentham.

The first attempt of Napoleon III, after the coup d'état, to promote a policy of public works was frustrated by the conservative financial ideas of the officials in charge, but in 1853 one of the most energetic of the prefects was brought to Paris. This was the Alsatian Protestant, Haussmann, who had hitched his administrative wagon to the rising star of Louis-Napoleon as early as the presidential election of 1848. As a godson of Prince Eugène, Haussmann had almost an hereditary claim to be regarded as a Bonapartist. Forceful and cunning, ambitious, unprincipled, formidable in bulk and character, he was the ideal agent for the Second Empire in a grade a little lower than the highest. He was to be Prefect of the Seine from 1853 to 1870. Such a man did not shrink from unorthodox, but up to a point justified, financial methods. The theory behind them was simply that the new values created by the reconstruction of the older sectors of Paris would themselves pay for the work that had to be undertaken.

The scope of Haussmann's demolition and reconstruction is amazing. He gave Paris eighty-five miles of new streets with wide carriageways and pavements shaded with trees. Private enterprise lined them with houses and shops, to a height and with a façade prescribed by the authorities, and in a style that represented Haussmann's idea of architectural beauty, for the Prefect of the Seine had the born philistine's conviction of his own impeccable artistic taste. Viollet-le-Duc, apart from the injury he did to Notre-Dame, was kept out of the rebuilding of Paris by Haussmann, who was neither romantic nor medieval. His passion, like that of Napoleon I, was for vistas. The Place de l'Étoile looks very fine from the air: it is a pity that it is not normally seen from that angle. Napoleon III, indeed, reproached Haussmann that in his love of straight lines he neglected the needs of traffic. The new railway stations, for example, were left without adequate approaches.

The best things in the re-planning of Paris were due to the influence of Napoleon III. His memories of London inspired the creation of many squares and other open places. The Bois de Boulogne, which had been a rather dull royal forest, cut across by long straight avenues for the hunters, was given by the Emperor to the city. At the instigation of Morny a racecourse was created at Longchamps; it rapidly became a fashionable social resort, the profits on which largely paid for the transformation of the uninteresting *bois* into a landscaped park. A similar treatment was accorded to the Bois de Vincennes on the east of Paris. Napoleon III was also responsible for the construction of the Halles, the great central market, as a functional structure of metal and glass.

Apart from the long, straight roads he drove through Paris, and the vistas they afforded, Haussmann's greatest achievement was in the drainage of the city. The sewers of Paris before him are luridly described by Victor Hugo in *Les Misérables.* By the end of the Second Empire the visit, especially of the great sewer which Haussmann liked to call his Cloaca Maxima, was a tourist attraction. A further virtue of the sewers was that they had been built without tearing anything else down, for much of old Paris and many fine and historic buildings were sacrificed to make it a Second Empire city. A sentimental regret for what was lost, and even an aesthetic distaste for what replaced it, would neither, perhaps, be justified if a fine modern city with improved living conditions had been built. But the tradition of urbanism, the Florence of the Medici, the Paris of Louis XV, the Nancy of King Stanislaus, had now come down to the boulevard Malesherbes and the Place de l'Opéra. Behind the state-prescribed façades of Haussmann's streets the builders could put up what they liked, and often new and more imposing slums replaced the older and more picturesque ones. Running water was only supplied at the option of the owner of a building, who often decided that it was an unnecessary luxury, since it involved the payment of a water rate. The function of the grand new sewers must not be mistaken; they were to remove the rain-water from the streets and prevent flooding. Sanitary, or rather insanitary, refuse still had to be carted away by an army of men at night in the traditional fashion, or sunk in cesspits, or deposited illegally in streets and gardens. Another, equally unpleasant, aspect of the city was the large area taken up by decaying bodies. Haussmann is not to be blamed for this; his plans for a great municipal cemetery outside Paris were successfully resisted by those who were determined that when they could do no more mischief there alive, they should leave their dead bodies to pollute the air and drinking water of the city.

The attention that was paid to Paris was not given to its surroundings. The Wall of the Farmers General (on the line of the present outer ring of boulevards), with its sixty gates, was now no longer the effective limit of occupation. A shift of population was taking place to the large area between this wall and the fortifications of the Orleanist Monarchy. Railway works and factories attracted a suburban population; and many of those who continued to work in Paris were drawn outwards by the cheapness of living in what was becoming a huge, poverty-stricken, higgledy-piggledy encampment of shacks. However, in the great enterprise of Haussmann, good and bad were mixed up together, and his achievement suited his day and generation. Contemporaries who began by opposing and then by mocking his efforts, came to admire the results.

The crown of them all was to be the new Paris Opera, built by Charles Garnier, inspired by the eighteenth-century Bordeaux Opera, and calculated for the gratification of a society even richer and more luxurious than the eighteenth-century mercantile aristocracy of Bordeaux, as well as for a less chaste artistic taste than that of the age of Louis XV. Within and without, it was loaded with decoration in all the styles known to history. A separate carriage-way led into a private entrance to the imperial box, for Napoleon remembered the attempt by Orsini and the murder of the duc de Berry. A huge entrance hall and elaborate stairs, for the arrival and reception of foreign or French notabilities; a foyer for the circulation of the fashionable throng; an auditorium surrounded by boxes to preserve the privacy of wealth and rank or facilitate amorous intrigue; a stage as deep as the auditorium, on which the most grandiose spectacles could be presented—such was the Paris Opera, a worthy setting for the luxury and splendour of Second Empire society, where Napoleon III and his Empress might shine amidst the wealthiest nouveaux riches and the most beautiful courtesans of Paris. This was a dream picture: in 1871 the Opera was still unfinished. It was completed, with the constitutional laws of the Third Republic, in 1875.

The Second Empire was the real bourgeois monarchy, an age of plutocrats without the culture or taste of an eighteenth-century

Farmer General, of fashionable priests without the religious feeling of a Lamennais or a Lacordaire, of well-disciplined academics without the intellectual distinction of the Orleanist scholars, of glittering *demi-mondaines* whose possession was one of the chief forms of ostentatious expenditure and signs of worldly success. The fashionable painters and writers were even more insignificant than usual in modern times. Apart from Daumier's cartoons, Millet's paintings exhibiting the dignity of labor, and Courbet's bourgeois-shocking realism, the only painters of real distinction were the rebels of the Salon des Refusés in 1863 who, rejected by official art, founded the great impressionist school of the Third Republic. The most lasting artistic creations that belong properly to the Second Empire are the comedies of Labiche and the operettas of Offenbach. What was on a higher level represented either a survival of the romanticism of the early century, or a direct or implied protest against the new society and its standards. Victor Hugo, fulminating in exile from the Channel Isles, launched *Les Châtiments* against "Napoléon le Petit." The cult of realism that is associated with the Third Republic developed in fact under the Second Empire, which recognized its enmity when the publications of *Madame Bovary* and the *Fleurs du Mal* were prosecuted in 1857.

If we want to see the spirit of the Second Empire at its best and most triumphant, we must look at the Exhibition of 1855, organized in imitation of the Great Exhibition of 1851 in London, but representing nonetheless a genuine aspiration after economic progress and pride in the beginnings of achievement.

J. Salwyn Schapiro

HERALDS OF FASCISM: LOUIS-NAPOLEON BONAPARTE, STATESMAN

J. Salwyn Schapiro (b. 1879), a product of Columbia University, taught for forty years at C.C.N.Y., retiring in 1947 as Emeritus Professor of History. A noted teacher, Professor Schapiro reached additional thousands of American students through his widely adopted and justly popular textbook, Modern and Contemporary European History. *Schapiro's research interests have centered on the history and meaning of Liberalism. The following excerpt is taken from one of his many works on the subject,* Liberalism and the Challenge of Fascism, *written two years after his "retirement." The author perceives many overtones of twentieth-century fascism in the regime of the Second Empire.*

The Second Empire was no more a restoration of the First Empire than the rule of the Bourbons, after 1815, was a restoration of the Old Regime. Despite the trappings and fittings of its Napoleonic predecessor, with which the Second Empire adorned itself, its advent marked the appearance of something new in political systems and in political ideologies. The real significance of the Second Empire is greater today than when it flourished. The methods that it employed, the policies that it pursued, and the ideas that it proclaimed anticipated in a vague, incomplete way what is now known as "fascism." Like fascism, it arose from similar conditions. During the reign of Louis-Philippe the Industrial Revolution was fairly under way in France. In the transitional stage, from artisan manufacture to the factory system, economic dislocation resulted, which created widespread unemployment among the ruined craftsmen. The Industrial Revolution in France advanced rapidly enough to throw many out of work, but not rapidly enough to absorb them into the new industries. As a consequence, there was "an overwhelming mass of people without a career and a young generation without a future. . . . This was the chief reason for the constantly recurring agitations, the infinite source of public and private suffering."

Two generations later there was a historic parallel to the overthrow of the Second French Republic. In Italy, after the First World

War, a dangerous situation was created by the economic disorganization that followed the end of hostilities. There was widespread unemployment and the government did little to alleviate the evil conditions under which millions were suffering. Deep resentment among the Italian workers led them to give a ready ear to those who preached social revolution: socialists, syndicalists, and communists. The revolutionary temper of the embittered workers reached the boiling point in 1920, when they went on a general strike and seized the factories. Though the uprising quickly collapsed, there was great apprehension among the propertied classes, who feared that the seizure of the factories was but a rehearsal for a socialist revolution. And they consequently gave their powerful support to the movement, led by Mussolini, to establish a fascist dictatorship. France in 1848 strikingly resembled Italy in 1920. Fear that the "June Days" were but a rehearsal for a socialist revolution had impelled the propertied classes in France to rally behind Napoleon. Mussolini's March on Rome in 1922 paralleled Napoleon's coup d'état in 1851.

Like Mussolini, Napoleon puzzled and confused many of his contemporaries. Even the usually perspicacious and far-sighted De Tocqueville had no inkling of the real significance of Napoleon, of whom he held no high opinion. According to De Tocqueville, Napoleon's "intelligence was incoherent, confused, filled with great but ill-assorted thoughts, which he borrowed now from the examples of Napoleon, now from socialistic theories, sometimes from recollections of England, where he lived: very different, and often very contrary, sources." He was "naturally a dreamer and a visionary." And one could not be long in contact with him "without discovering a little vein of madness which was chiefly responsible for his success." The powerful interests that, openly or secretly, rallied to Napoleon's support had no great opinion of his ability or confidence in the strength of his character. What they wanted him to do was to eliminate the socialists from the political scene with a strong hand and then to become their pliant tool in the government of France. Again to quote the observant De Tocqueville, the politicians expected to find in Napoleon "an instrument which they could handle as they pleased, and which it would always be lawful for them to break when they wished to. In this, they were greatly deceived." Once in power, Napoleon swept aside the bourgeois politicians as ruthlessly as he suppressed the socialist revolutionists.

Nothing is easier than to find factual parallels in history. They are generally plausible, seldom convincing, and never instructive. To see the origins of great changes in history is a quite different—and more important—matter. As nature abhors a vacuum, history abhors changes without origins, whether immediate or remote. Fascism did not spring fully grown from the chin of Mussolini. It had historic origins, not so much in Italy itself as in France, which since the French Revolution has furnished many revolutionary patterns to Latin Europe.

The organization and policies of the Second Empire bore startling resemblances to the fascist dictatorships of our time. It was a dictatorship based on popular support, as expressed in plebiscites and in "elections." Napoleon realized what neither the Bourbons nor Louis-Philippe had realized: that popular support was all essential in maintaining a government in post-revolutionary France. To obtain popular support he established a parliament, the *Corps législatif,* elected by manhood suffrage. The acid test of parliamentary government is the existence of an opposition that arises from free elections and that aims to assume power. No real parliamentary opposition existed throughout the period of the Second Empire. The method of "official candidates," already established by the Bourbons and perfected into a system by the July Monarchy, concerned a small electorate, which was easily controlled. Under the Second Empire this system was applied thoroughly and efficiently to the huge electorate that came with manhood suffrage, punctiliously maintained by Napoleon. Official candidates were put in nomination in every district by a smoothly running political machine, organized by the government. For a time few, if any, opposition candidates appeared. Under the Second Empire there was a false majority in parliament, elected by manhood suffrage, as there had been false majorities in the parliaments of the Bourbon and Orleanist monarchies, which had been elected by small groups of property owners. As in the fascist dictatorships, the voters under the Second Empire went to the polls, not to elect representatives, but to endorse the list of candidates drawn up by the government; and parliament met, not to pass laws, but to ratify decrees presented by the government. In fact, though not in theory, elections were conducted on a one-party basis. It took a bold and courageous man to oppose the official candidate; an opposition candidate at the elections was sure to arouse the vindictive enmity of the government. Few dared to assume such a risk. In 1857 the government presented for reelection all the members of the outgoing parliament. This complete flouting of the democratic process created widespread resentment which found expression in the election of five opposition candidates. *Les cinq,* as the opponents of the government were known, constituted the beginning of a parliamentary opposition, which grew in numbers during the last decade of the Second Empire.

Public opinion in France, as expressed in the press, was traditionally anti-government. Napoleon conceived the idea of having the entire press used as the mouthpiece of the government, an idea later applied in the fascist dictatorships. A highly organized censorship controlled, cajoled, directed, or terrorized the newspapers into becoming organs of the government. Opposition newspapers were suppressed, and their editors jailed or exiled. Suppression of opposition newspapers was not a new thing in postrevolutionary France. What was new was the systematic use of the entire press to give the illusion that public opinion supported the government. Like manhood suffrage, the press was an integral part of the new type of dictatorship, which boasted of being the expression of the popular will.

What did the "socialist Emperor" do about labor? To allay the bourgeois terror of a class struggle between labor and capital, trade unions were outlawed and strikes forbidden. In 1853 the government inaugurated a method of labor-capital cooperation through a system of industrial councils representing both sides. To these councils, *conseils des prud'hommes,* was given the task of regulating wages, hours, and conditions in the factories. Such bodies had existed before, but under the Second Empire they were used by the government to support its labor policies. Frequently men not even connected with the industry were appointed by the authorities as officials of the *conseils.* As a system, the *conseils* suggested the Nazi Labor Front, in that they were intermediary groups between the workers and the government, under the political direction of the latter and used as a means of controlling the former. What the Emperor desired, writes a latter-day apologist of Napoleon, was "to create an army of workers of the same type as that created by the National Socialists in Germany a century later."

Another way of controlling the workers was through the *livret.*

In 1854 a law made more stringent the regulations of this industrial passport in order to enable the police to keep watch over the comings and goings of the workers. Since the "June Days" there was a great dread of the Paris worker, who was regarded as the uncompromising enemy of the social order, ever ready to overthrow it by mass insurrection. A secret report on the attitude of the working class, made by a government agent, asserted that the worker was a socialist, as, before 1789, the bourgeois had been a *philosophe*. "The bourgeois sought to establish a system that they could use as a weapon against the dominance of the nobility and the clergy. The worker now favors a system which he can use to overthrow, if possible, all inequalities." During the Second Empire the workers, cowed by repressive measures, were silent, industrious, and, to all appearances, submissive. Despite the great advance of industry during the regime of Napoleon, the condition of the mass of workers did not improve greatly. It was estimated that there were then in France about three million paupers and about six million who were often in a condition below the poverty line.

What did Napoleon do to advance social reform, which had been the burden of his appeal to the workers? Very little. He did nothing at all to establish the agricultural colonies that he had advocated so fervently in his *De l'extinction du paupérisme*. Government subventions were given to associations having for their object old-age pensions and sickness insurance. To diminish unemployment, the government instituted *les grands travaux,* public works of which the rebuilding of Paris was the most famous project. The social reforms of the Second Empire were meager performances, considering the generous promises that the Emperor had made when he was bidding for power.

The class that benefited most from the Second Empire was the bourgeoisie. Napoleon had learned from his early associates, the disciples of Saint-Simon, that a new historic era had come with the Industrial Revolution. Thenceforth, the capitalists, not the aristocrats, were to be the ruling class in society. The chief aim of the Saint-Simonians was the economic development of France. They were little interested in political rights and in popular government, and generally subordinated political to economic questions. If any intellectual group could be said to have been the mentors of the Second Empire, it was the Saint-Simonians. Closely associated with the government in its various economic enterprises were Michel Chevalier, the brothers Péreire, and Père Enfantin—all disciples of the famous Utopian socialist.

Napoleon did all in his power to encourage commerce and industry, which won for the government the powerful support of the new moneyed class. Anti-Semitism played no part in the Emperor's policies, despite its upflare during his campaign for the presidency; the Jewish bankers, the Rothschild family, and the brothers Péreire were very influential in government finance. The pace of industrialization in France after 1815 had been slow, hampered in part by aristocratic indifference, in part by social agitation. During the Second Empire, France was in a fever of business enterprise and machine production. Two new financial institutions, the *Crédit foncier* and the *Crédit mobilier,* financed the building of the great railway system of France, the rebuilding of Paris, and the organization of the French Line operating trans-Atlantic steamships. Railway mileage increased sixfold during the period of the Second Empire. Steel production was greatly increased by the expansion of the steel plant at Le Creusot. The horsepower of machines used in industry quintupled. France was beginning to catch up with England in the rapid development of modern industry.

In his economic as well as in his political policies, reconciliation was the watchword of Napoleon III. He desired to reconcile capital with labor; authoritative government with manhood suffrage; and a rigid censorship with a free press. The prime motive of his reconciliation policy was to solve the as yet unsolved problem of the two Frances. Napoleon fully realized the vital importance of the problem, as well as the failure of the different political groups to solve it. The French Revolution, he declared, "had two distinct characteristics—one social, the other political. The social revolution has triumphed in spite of our reverses, while the political one has failed in spite of the victories of the people. That is the cause of all our discomfort now." He came to the conclusion that all efforts to bring unity to France had failed because they had all been partisan in character: legitimist, bourgeois liberal, or republican. Because he belonged to none of these parties, insisted Napoleon, he was best fitted to unite the two Frances. He would do so by a plan that incorporated the fundamental principle of each political element. From the legitimists he would take the monarchical principle, by establishing a new dynasty. From the bourgeois liberals he would take the parliamentary principle, by establishing a representative body. From the republicans he would take the principle of popular sovereignty, by maintaining manhood suffrage. He would reassure the propertied classes by suppressing socialist revolts. To reassure the workers, "Saint-Simon on horseback," as Napoleon was called, would institute social reforms for the welfare of the masses. This uniting of the various conflicting elements would *terminer enfin la Révolution française,* and the two Frances at last would become one.

There was to be a guarantee of this unity: authoritarian government. The dictatorial rule of Napoleon was carried out with great firmness. Thousands of recalcitrant republicans were exiled or imprisoned or were compelled to flee. The most famous of these new *émigrés* was Victor Hugo, whose denunciation of the Emperor and of his system was immortalized in his books *Napoléon-le-Petit* and *Histoire d'un crime.* All expressions of public opinion hostile to the Emperor, in the press, in popular assemblies, and in the schools, were ruthlessly suppressed. The famous historians Michelet and Quinet were ousted from their academic chairs. The Legitimists and the Orleanists, less recalcitrant, were ignored. The church was cajoled into supporting the regime by the *loi Falloux* and by the encouragement given to the clergy. Napoleon was assiduous in showing deference to Catholic opinion by government support of Catholic societies, schools, and charities. Though the regime of the Second Empire was not "totalitarian" in the fascist sense, almost every institution in the land felt the hand of the government, which regulated, prescribed, punished, and suppressed opinions and activities that were hostile to Napoleon.

Did the Napoleonic dictatorship succeed in solving the persistent problem of uniting the two Frances? It certainly seemed so. All through the period of the Second Empire domestic peace reigned in France; no uprisings, no strikes of any consequence, and no serious parliamentary opposition disquieted the government. The nation appeared to be united behind the Emperor, who, toward the end of his reign, received an almost unanimous vote of confidence as a result of a plebiscite. But appearances belied the realities of the situation in France. On the morrow of the fall of the Empire there broke out the bloodiest uprising in the revolutionary history of France—the Paris Commune. Dictatorship had not been a solution.

In an extraordinary, penetrating pamphlet, *De l'esprit de conquête et de l'usurpation,* Benjamin Constant gave an analysis of the methods used by a dictator in ruling a nation. What he said referred to Napoleon I, but it applied even more forcefully to the methods used by Napoleon III. "The existence of public sentiment," he wrote, "being dangerous to dictatorship and the semblance of public sentiment being necessary to it, the dictatorship strikes the people with one hand to stifle any real sentiment; and it strikes them again with the other hand to compel them to act as if motivated by public sentiment." When a dictator "condemns innocence, he includes calumny so that his action will seem to be justified." When he decides on a policy, the dictator orders "a ridiculous investigation to serve as a prelude to what he had decided to do. This counterfeit liberty combines all the evils of anarchy and slavery. There is no end to a tyranny which seeks to drag forth tokens of consent. Peaceable men are persecuted for indifference, energetic men, for being dangerous." Dictatorship invents a falsified popular approval of the government; and the result is that fear "comes to ape all the appearances of courage, to congratulate itself on dishonor, and to give thanks for unhappiness." Dictatorship resorts to the practice of hiring corrupt journalists who parody freedom of the press. They "argue, as though trying to convince; they fly into a passion as though fighting an opposition; they fling insults as though there was any chance of replying." Under a despotic monarchy, the people are enslaved; but under a dictatorship, they are also degraded. A dictatorship "debases a people while oppressing them, and accustoms them to trample under foot what they once respected, to court what they once scorned, and even to scorn themselves."

Nazi writers in Germany have evaluated the historic importance of Napoleon as a harbinger of fascism, despite the marked differences between the Second Empire and the Third Reich. A book, *Masse oder Volk,* written by Konstantin Frantz in 1852, was republished in 1933 with a significant preface by the Nazi Franz Kemper. "The rise to power of Louis-Napoleon," wrote Kemper, "is the only historical parallel to the National Socialist revolution of our day." According to Frantz, the Napoleonic state depended on mass support, without which it could not be maintained even by the powerful Imperial army. Only through social reform could the danger of socialism be eliminated. In the view of another Nazi writer, Michael Freund, Napoleon was the only real revolutionist in 1848. "After the solemn republican respectability of 1848 it seemed that only with the Napoleonic experiment did a great revolutionary élan appear on the stage of history." The state created by Napoleon was antisocialist, but it was not the laissez-faire state of capitalism. The social ideals of the disciples of Saint-Simon were given by Napoleon, for the first time, a military and authoritarian aspect. Still another Nazi, K. H. Bremer, diagnosed the situation of the Second Republic in the following manner. While the republicans of 1848 were trying to solve the constitutional question, he observed, Napoleon realized that the social question was the most important one. Parliamentarism, with its conflicting political parties and class struggles, was incapable of solving the social question. Only a dictatorship with a social outlook, in the view of Napoleon, could solve it. His great aim was to establish a political system based upon the unity of all classes and of all interests in France. It was he, according to Bremer, who first created the new type of state in the form of authoritarian, plebiscitarian leadership.

The prefascist pattern of Napoleon's dictatorship collapsed even before Sedan. What was called the "Liberal Empire," inaugurated in 1867, marked a definite trend toward liberalism. Elections became freer, and opposition parties appeared in parliament. The control of the press was relaxed. Public meetings were more freely permitted. Even more significant were the concessions made to the workers. Trade-unions were legalized, collective bargaining was recognized, and strikes were permitted.

What caused this transition from the fascist pattern of the dictatorship to the pattern of the "Liberal Empire"? Rising discontent among powerful elements in the nation forced Napoleon to make concessions to liberalism. The protectionists opposed his reciprocity treaty with England. The Catholics opposed his alliance with the Italian nationalists in the Austro-Sardinian war. The liberals loudly demanded a return to constitutional government and the restoration of "the necessary liberties." The disastrous failure of the Emperor's intervention in Mexico brought the discontented elements together in a common hostility to the Empire. Napoleon sought to ward off by timely concessions a revolutionary upheaval such as had overtaken his predecessor, Louis-Philippe; hence, *l'Empire libéral.*

These explanations, while true enough, merely indicate the weakness of the Second Empire as a fascist experiment. Neither Hitler nor Mussolini made any concessions to liberalism throughout their dictatorships. *The weakness of the fascist pattern of Napoleon lay in that it did not include totalitarianism.* Napoleon never attempted "to coordinate" the political, economic, and social life of France into a uniform, unified, national system, run by a dictatorial machine. He would not have succeeded had he tried to do so. There were serious obstacles to totalitarianism in the France of his day. Despite fairly rapid industrial advance during the Second Empire, France continued to be primarily an agricultural nation. Land was cultivated by millions of peasant proprietors, passionately individualistic, who would quickly have resented any abrogation of their rights as independent cultivators. There did not then exist large combinations of basic industries, which easily lend themselves to government control and regulation. French industry generally was based on small competitive units that could not be "coordinated" even by the most despotic of dictatorships. Neither was there a large working class, organized in powerful trade-unions, that could be taken over and directed by a dictatorship. Totalitarianism requires, in addition, easy and rapid means of communication and transportation, such as radio, motion pictures, automobiles, and airplanes, which a dictatorship can use for propaganda purposes. It also requires a national school system in which the masses of the people can be indoctrinated with a common ideology. France of the mid-nineteenth century had none of these means of "coordination." Had Napoleon attempted to do what Hitler did so quickly and so successfully, the revolutionary tocsin would have been heard in every hamlet and in every quarter of France.

The social experiment of the dictatorship of Napoleon is the most significant aspect of the Second Empire. It has been obscured by the sensational foreign policies of the Emperor, which led to the Crimean, the Austro-Sardinian, and the Franco-Prussian wars, and finally to his dramatic downfall. In the light of fascism, it can now be discerned that a new political method of fighting social revolution had been devised, namely, to turn the revolutionary stream of working-class discontent into the new channel of a popular and socialized dictatorship. Napoleon's pioneer fascism failed, and its failure discredited the newly-born legend of "Saint-Simon on horseback." It also discredited militarism, with which the experiment was so closely linked. The downfall of the Second Empire exploded the "Napoleonic legend" so violently that even Napoleon I was struck by the flying missiles. The great Napoleon, as well as *Napoléon le Petit,* now appeared to the French as an "architect of ruin." Waterloo and Sedan became joined, in popular opinion, as the outstanding national disasters in the history of France.

Strangely enough, bourgeois liberalism also was discredited by the Second Empire. The social experiments of Napoleon, however tentative and halting, and the maintenance of manhood suffrage, however illusory and ineffective, yet kept alive a democratic sentiment in France. A restoration of bourgeois liberalism, with its neglect of the working class and with its capitalist rule, was as distasteful after 1870 as the restoration of the Bourbons had been after 1815. If it did nothing else, the Second Empire had accustomed the French people to think of government in its intimate relationship with their everyday problems. Was it possible to establish a new government on a truly democratic basis—one that would concern itself chiefly with the welfare of the masses? Such a government, of necessity, would be a republic, in order that it repudiate, at the same time, the bourgeois liberalism of the July Monarchy and the dictatorship of the Second Empire. It would have to make a powerful appeal for national unity, in order to face the grave problems that arose as a consequence of the defeat of France in the Franco-Prussian War. Would a democratic republic close the chasm that, for so long, had divided the two Frances? Out of these necessities was born the Third French Republic.

Theodore Zeldin

THE MYTH OF NAPOLEON III

Theodore Zeldin (b. 1933), Lecturer in Modern History at Oxford University, Fellow of St. Antony's College, is one of the younger English specialists in French history. His first book, The Political System of Napoleon III *(1958), immediately brought him to the front rank of the revisionists. In the following article, originally published in* History Today, *Mr. Zeldin states that the standing of Napoleon III as a statesman "must depend to a very considerable extent on the way in which the Liberal Empire is interpreted." While there is no denying the validity of this criterion, the verdict rendered in its light is one about which historians might and have honestly continued to differ.*

"Read no history, nothing but biography, for that is life without theory." So Disraeli once said, but it is not a maxim that can be applied to Napoleon III. His life contained so many adventures, conspiracies, and love affairs, his court was so well provided with gossip and intrigue, his career reached such depths and such heights of fortune, that it is no wonder that his biographers have not had time to stop to ask what he achieved as a statesman. They would have been surprised to know that he was, in the opinion of Lamartine, the greatest politician France had had since Talleyrand, and possibly even greater than he.

It is not from any personal animosity that they refuse to treat him seriously. On the contrary, for it can be said of few, as it can be said of him, that no one who ever knew him detested him or even found him disagreeable. His gift for making friends was quite extraordinary, and even his bitterest enemies concede that he was an amiable man. That in fact, is how they damn him. He was a pleasant man, they say, with good intentions, no doubt, but with no political gifts and with none of the ability necessary to carry out his grandiose schemes. He was a rake, an adventurer, a dreamer, a charlatan, but nothing like his uncle, of course.

He ended as he began, in exile, and his critics have enjoyed showing that his failure was inevitable. He gradually divested himself of much of his power; and they have assumed that he did so because he was compelled to yield before the growing strength of the oppo-

From Theodore Zeldin, "The Myth of Napoleon III," *History Today*, 8 (February 1958). Reprinted by permission of *History Today* and Theodore Zeldin.

sition, and decided to give up his control of the state in order to retain his throne. His Liberal Empire collapsed after little more than a hundred days; and they have assumed that it was a mere epilogue to his reign and not the consummation of his work. His government did not include the old parliamentary leaders; and they have asserted, therefore, that his supporters were mere nonentities and henchmen. They enjoy quoting the pretty phrase attributed to him: "The Empress is legitimist, my cousin is republican, Morny is Orleanist, I am a socialist: the only Bonapartist is Persigny and he is mad"; and from this they conclude that the Second Empire represented nothing but a jumble of second-hand ideas. Some claim that it was established almost accidentally, under the influence of force and excitement, that it had no real roots in the country, and that its motto should have been not "Liberty, Equality and Fraternity" but that given to it by Marx, "Cavalry, Infantry and Artillery."

It is extraordinary how reputations are made and unmade in history. The great achievements of Castlereagh, for example, were condemned to a hundred years of oblivion very largely by the superior wit of his rival Canning and by the famous phrase of Byron; and likewise, under the influence of his royalist successors, Oliver Cromwell was spurned as a bigot and a tyrant for twice that time, until his letters and speeches were published to show what he was really like. In the other direction, it is well-known how Napoleon I looked after his own reputation and how he created the legend about himself which made his name into a positive political force. After Waterloo, he became the martyr of St. Helena, whence he preached the gospel of his own glory, proclaiming the excellence of his intentions and encouraging posterity to forget everything in his reign that was not to his credit. His political enemies were in power for a bare fifteen years. Louis-Philippe erected monuments to his glory and brought his ashes back to France as those of a national hero. Napoleon III gave him another twenty years of official worship, published his correspondence in fifty volumes and so made it impossible for anyone ever to deny his greatness. His reputation never had to contend seriously with popular hostility or ignorance.

Exactly the opposite happened to Napoleon III. His martyrdom in the fortress of Ham took place before his reign; and though it helped him to gain his throne, it came too early to influence historical opinion. In 1873 he planned to repeat the return from Elba, but died before he could do so. The literary world was largely hostile to him and vilified him as *Napoléon le Petit*. The two best histories of his reign are by a republican and a royalist, and the French school textbooks have long reflected the views of his political enemies, who obtained the professorships after his fall. He has, indeed, never been allowed to speak for himself: his published correspondence barely fills a few volumes and most of it dates from his early days of exile. There is nothing resembling the huge series on his uncle to show what he was really like as a ruler.

There has thus grown up a myth about Napoleon III as a sort of counterpart to the legend about Napoleon I. It began with the story that he had been elected president because the royalist politicians thought he would be a tool in their hands, a story that they invented to flatter their own importance. There is, in fact, incontrovertible evidence that they supported him because they saw that he was bound to win; and Thiers, who never erred on the side of modesty, would have stood himself had he thought he had any chance at all. The story that he was allowed to take his seat in parliament in June 1848 because he was considered harmless and an imbecile is also an invention from the same source. Rumors were spread that he could not speak French, that his hobby was rearing eagles in cages, that so conscious was he of his own incompetence that he had opened negotiations of his own accord to secure the return of the legitimist pretender. The politicians who met him, however, quickly saw how wide all this propaganda was of the truth. Montalembert, the leader of the liberal Catholics, was much impressed when he first went to see him in October, 1848. "I cannot conceive," he noted in his diary, "where his reputation for incompetence comes from."

It is time, therefore, that the abuse of his enemies should be appreciated in its true light and not accepted as impartial history merely because they happened to be distinguished men. What has been said about him should be put aside and an attempt should be made to study the facts and the primary sources. The man, however, cannot be assessed unless his work is also assessed, and that is why biography without history is not enough for him.

His standing as a statesman must depend to a very considerable extent on the way in which the Liberal Empire is interpreted. Napoleon I claimed in exile that his object had always been to establish liberty, and that the Hundred Days were destined to inaugurate a new era of peace and constitutional monarchy. No one has believed him, and quite rightly, for his character and his career made it impossible for him to accomplish such a metamorphosis. Is it right, however, to dismiss the similar claims of Napoleon III? Was he a liberal only in opposition and a despot as soon as he got the reins of power into his own hands?

In truth, he was probably a determined believer in the merits of neither liberalism nor despotism, but an opportunist above all else. He had thought a great deal about the art of success, and he was determined not to repeat the mistakes that had made others, and especially his uncle, fail before him. Politics was for him "the application of history." The task of the statesman was to study history and to discover which of the driving forces in the world had passed forever and which would triumph. Success would come to him who judged correctly which way the wind was blowing and trimmed his sails accordingly; to him who always made sure to lead events and not to be dragged by them. He must represent the aspirations of his epoch; and that is why his flatttering courtiers pleased him by saying, "Sire, you are the century."

"In the end," he once declared, "it is always public opinion that wins the last victory." He concluded from his study of history, and in particular from his study of the history of England, the most successful of monarchies, that "It is not chance that determines the destinies of nations; it is not an unforeseen accident that overthrows or maintains thrones. There is a general cause that determines events and makes them follow logically from each other. A government can often violate law and even liberty with impunity, but if it does not put itself openly at the head of the great interests of civilization, it can have only an ephemeral existence." He would always seek to give the French what they wanted.

In 1848 he was, to an extraordinary extent, "the man of the century"; and he did not owe his success simply to the attraction of his name. He represented better than anyone else the French peasantry, whose hearts were on the left but whose pockets were on the right, who were fond of being "advanced" in theory but who, in the practical conduct of life, sought only the traditional rewards for their labor—property and social advancement for their children. Similarly, Napoleon was at once conservative and radical, a lover of peace but also a lover of glory, an unbeliever married to a religious wife—a bundle of contradictions, but of the very contradictions that were innate in the great majority of his subjects.

He was the only politician of the time who could be conservative without being retrograde. The proclamation of universal suffrage had cast terror into the old parliamentary leaders who hastened to modify and limit it as soon as they returned to power. Napoleon alone knew how to place himself at the head of such an electorate, to lead it in the direction he chose and so to prove that it could be a perfectly harmless and conservative force. When he fell in 1870, no one could seriously think of abolishing universal suffrage; and this is not the least of his contributions to the development of the institutions of his country.

He consolidated universal suffrage rather in the way that Sir Robert Walpole and the Pelhams had consolidated parliamentary monarchy in England. They had made the king's government work by giving the House of Commons and the gentry what they wanted, by providing pasture enough for all the hungry beasts in politics and by following a policy that was popular with the nation. So likewise Napoleon made his government work by offering the electorate what it wanted, in return for support on matters to which it was indifferent. The centralization of Louis XIV and Napoleon I placed immense power in the hands of the government, and without the approval or initiative of its head very little could be done. Napoleon III argued that the details of politics mattered little to the peasants, and that they did not care whether there were one or two parliaments in Paris or none at all. He thought that what really interested them was how to finance improvements in their daily existence, how to build roads to their farms and railways to their markets, how to bring water to their villages and how to establish local schools for their children, and how, on top of all this, to find the money to maintain their hospitals and their almshouses, to repair their churches and to embellish their village halls. The centralization of the country required the peasants to pay taxes for these very purposes, but they had to send their money to Paris and then to beg it back from the government. The government was willing to help those who helped it. It redistributed the taxes in the form of subsidies to the villages that voted favorably in the elections. It offered part as a bait, just before the elections, and the rest as a reward if the results were satisfactory. It seemed a good bargain to many who cared nothing for politics and hence the unanimous votes which the opposition attributed to force.

A good deal of force and intimidation was, of course, used but not on the great majority of ordinary men. The system was more subtle than that. Napoleon had by far the best organized party in the country, for he had at his disposal the civil service, which now reached the zenith of its prestige and its power. The prefects, enjoying their heyday and reproducing in the provinces the glitter of the imperial court, were not simply administrators but the veritable political leaders of their departments. They gave much time to the task of making converts to Bonapartism, wooing the aristocracy with dinner parties and balls, wooing the bourgeoisie with jobs and favors, wooing above all the masses with the gift and the promise of material benefits. They took the credit for the prosperity that the country enjoyed; and it is largely thanks to them that the Second Empire was afterwards remembered as the good old days when men used to play games with golden coins.

They could speak to almost every peasant in the country through the mayors of the villages, appointed by the government and so invested with all the authority that comes from being an official of a centralized state like France. These mayors presided over the elections in the villages; and they made sure that the people understood the "social contract" of the Second Empire. They did not compel any man to vote for Napoleon or his official candidates, and they did not falsify the returns of unanimous results: they just made it unwise to cast a contrary vote. The system of voting was different from that now used in England. The voter was not presented with a list of candidates and asked to place a cross against one of them. Instead, he was required to put in the box a ballot paper which he had to produce himself, bearing the name of his favorite. These ballot papers were generally supplied by the candidates; but the government had the advantage that it sent the ballot paper of the candidate it supported with the card that entitled an elector to vote. The ignorant, therefore, frequently came to vote with their electoral cards and their government ballot papers, which they put in the box as though they were the only ones that could be used. When some poor peasant came to the village hall with a ballot paper that an opposition agent had given him, the mayor presiding over the box would at once spot it.

"Ah!" he would say. "Haven't you got any other ballot paper apart from that one?"

"Why, yes, Monsieur le Maire."

"Show me."

The elector shows several. The mayor takes the official candidate's and says, "Here, my good man, this is the *good one;* put the others down—." Then the mayor puts it into the box. Or he would say, "Put the ballot paper you've got into your pocket and take this one: this is the *good one.*"

Such proceedings took place when the mayor was a paternal figure and the elector a submissive peasant. But sometimes a more arrogant man would march into the voting hall and demand a ballot paper. He is given the official candidate's. He asks for "another one." The mayor says there are no others. The man insists. The mayor gets angry. A row would start and in the end the man would probably be thrown out. Of course, the mayor would receive great sympathy; for was not this desire to vote against his advice a challenge to his authority, a doubt cast upon his knowledge of how administrative business should be transacted? It was for personal reasons, as much as because of their political preferences, that the mayors lost their tempers with organizers of opposition. They looked upon dissent as a personal insult. One mayor, no more pompous than most, thus writes to his prefect: "Yesterday three men travelled over my commune, putting up red posters everywhere in favor of M. Casimir Perier. When I and a gendarme asked them by what right they were putting up notices on the wall of the town hall without my authorization, they replied in an impertinent manner, that they had no need of my authorization." This was a slur on his dignity and his rage can be imagined.

The mayors had valuable allies in the schoolmasters, who were likewise agents of the state. Here is a report from one of them to show how they acted: "As secretary of the town hall, entrusted in this capacity with the preparation of all the election documents, I was able to exercise far greater influence on the elections. In conjunction with the village constable, I distributed the ballot papers I received from Monsieur le Préfet to the electors. I strongly supported the candidature of M. Arnaud, the government's candidate. I tried to make the electors understand that we must all without exception consolidate the plans of our august Emperor by a unanimous vote. Despite this, I was compelled to redouble my zeal and energy owing to the fact that some agitators had led astray a large number of electors and particularly twenty electors at a village not far away, who had been earnestly solicited to vote for M. Dupont Delporte and were completely disposed to vote for the latter and in consequence to reject the government's candidate. Having heard this vexatious news, I went to make them see the error into which they had fallen. To prove to them that the government is good, I gave them knowledge of a letter which Monsieur le Maire of the commune had received from Monsieur le Préfet, in which it is said that a new subsidy of 220,000 francs had just been given to the department to be divided between the communes that had suffered in the floods of 1856. In the presence of this testimony of the solicitude of the government, will you be so ungrateful, I told them, as to refuse it your co-operation: and at once they all threw down the ballot papers that had been given to them and came at once to the town hall to vote for M. Arnaud."

In the course of the reign this system gradually disintegrated, and by 1869 it had pretty well collapsed. Napoleon himself hastened its collapse by his own measures. He found it unsatisfactory despite, and even because of, the almost absolute power that it gave him. One day, talking with the duc de Plaisance of his days as president of the republic, he said regretfully, "Ah! Those were the days!" Plaisance said things did not seem to have worsened for him. "You are quite wrong, my dear duke," replied Napoleon. "At that time it was all life and movement around me; today it is silence. I am isolated, I no longer hear anything." He was expected to do everything himself, but inevitably, in practice, he could not. He had to bear all the responsibility, nevertheless, while his ministers wielded their immense power without adequate control from parliament or from each other. Both he and they soon perceived that such checks were desirable, quite apart from any ideological reasons, simply in the interests of more efficient government. He saw, too, that he could hardly go on preaching liberty to the rulers of Europe when he did not practice it himself. He was getting old, moreover; and yet as things stood, all the achievements of the reign hung on the life of one sick man. He must provide for the future and found institutions that would render his work permanent.

Many of his earliest supporters had no wish to continue with the old system either. They may have been docile enough when he emerged clothed in all the prestige that his immense victories at the plebiscites gave him; but now they thought it was time they should share his power. They could no longer win their elections in their constituencies simply by declaring their loyalty to him, by saying, as did an old veteran of Waterloo, "If you re-elect me, I shall, as before, support the Empire and we will repeat together 'Long Live The Emperor.'" They now had to meet the powerful challenge of an opposition which promised all the utopian joys the age could imagine. They could no longer defeat them by the old system; so they had to outdo them at their own game and promise even more, with liberty to crown it. In this way did they become supporters of a Liberal Empire, which was thus created not by the opponents of Napoleon but by his old supporters, converted like him. They had the good fortune to find in Emile Ollivier a leader who had one of the rarest and most elevated minds of his day, and who was able to organize them and to bring their vague ambitions to success.

The Liberal Empire was an attempt to break the vicious circle of revolution and reaction in which France had been caught since Louis XVI. It sought to effect progress without revolution, in the belief that reforms could be obtained only gradually, whereas revolutions, being essentially violent, would never achieve their ends because they inevitably created new problems and brought divisions, emigrations, and reaction in their train. It held that France could not turn at once from despotism to parliamentary government; and it established a representative form of government as a first step. It was not muddled thinking that led it to maintain that if France wished to imitate nineteenth-century England, she should first start by copying her neighbor's preliminary institutions of the seventeenth and eighteenth centuries.

It is possible to argue therefore that since Napoleon III tackled, and for a time successfully solved, the most fundamental problem in French politics, he can claim a place among the great statesmen of the century. When the prejudice against him has died down, it will very likely be recognized that he came near to achieving as much in politics as his uncle achieved in administration and in war.

IV CONCLUSION: SOME OVERALL EVALUATIONS

Pierre de La Gorce
NAPOLEON THE WELL-MEANING

Pierre de La Gorce (1846–1934), a Catholic of moderate royalist leanings, was one of the first French historians to approach the Second Empire with scholarly detachment. His seven-volume Histoire du Second Empire *(1894–1905) remains the standard work on the subject.* Napoléon III et sa Politique, *from which the following excerpts are taken, was published in 1934, shortly before La Gorce's death and almost thirty years after the completion of his magnum opus. This selection thus represents the mature and ultimate judgment of a distinguished scholar who devoted many years and considerable talent to the study of Napoleon III and the Second Empire.*

I would like to describe, without any attempt at chronological coverage, the principal characteristics of this most complex man. His most distinctive traits were secretiveness and stubbornness. Everything in his childhood had taught him to shroud himself in mystery. After 1815, a kind of international police had kept a close watch on the Bonapartes: visits, excursions, trips—all were duly noted. Under such circumstances, one tends to try to hide everything. Louis Bonaparte learned early to cover up his tracks, and he was later to resort to dissimulation in situations when it served no purpose whatsoever. For Louis-Napoleon, who was instinctively attracted by clandestine activities, Italy, the classic land of secret societies, was a training ground. He endorsed the Italian cause with more ardor than wisdom. The warm, but compromising friends he made there were later to remind him of the pledges and ties of an earlier day.

To conspire for others is to learn to conspire for oneself. However, the coups attempted at Strasbourg and Boulogne were those of a novice who still had a lot to learn. Prison bars failed to dampen a vivid imagination, and, in fact, the years at the Fortress of Ham merely served to whet the Prince's fondness for plots. The first to hatch was a plan of escape, and he made good his bid for freedom, to the amusement of the populace, whose interest in jailbreaks is insatiable.

Once President of the Republic, the prisoner of Ham continued

From Pierre de La Gorce, *Napoleon III et sa Politique* (Paris, 1933). Used by permission of Librairie Plon. All rights reserved. Editor's translation.

to conspire. But this latest plot, pitting the chief executive against the Legislative Assembly, showed signs of experience and maturity. No intrigue was ever more carefully woven. Louis Bonaparte's first ministers—Odilon Barrot, Tocqueville, Falloux—were much more the Deputies' men than his own. He quietly redistributed the portfolios, less intent on forming a tight-knit administration than in dominating a cabinet staffed with sycophants. Yet, while gradually obtaining greater freedom of action, he was careful not to break with the parliamentary leaders. He was at once docile and evasive in his relations with them, and although the balance of power had shifted to his side he still assumed the attitude of a disciple. A true conspirator will emerge from the shadows from time to time, and by unmasking himself in a feigned display of candor will do much to assure the success of his machinations. Once, at Saint-Quentin he declared in an outburst of democratic fervor that "his true friends lived not in palaces, but under thatched roofs." Another time, at Lyon, he paid an emotional tribute to popular sovereignty. On still another occasion, at Caen, without taking it out of the scabbard —that would have ruined everything—he rattled the sword of Napoleon: "In a time of crisis, should the people want to delegate new powers to the head of state, his refusal to accept this sacred mission would be tantamount to desertion." After such outbursts, Louis Bonaparte reverted to long periods of silence; while the Assembly continued to wear itself out in endless debates.

The conflict between the two branches was marked by truces like that resulting from the conciliatory address of November 12, 1850. Yet each truce was followed by a widening of the breach. Two months after the aforementioned address, for instance, Changarnier, the Assembly's chief defender, was removed from the command of the Army of Paris. A revision of the Constitution proroguing the President's powers would have removed the need and the temptation of an outright usurpation. Yet the Assembly refused to approve the proposed amendment. The conspiracy then entered the critical stage. The plotters worked almost openly, and the danger signs were visible to the naked eye. The threatened Assembly tried to organize a counterplot. But could five hundred deputies hope to conspire effectively? Napoleon's task was twofold: to enlist the support of the people, and to rally the bourgeoisie. He lured the first with a promise to reestablish universal suffrage without any residence qualifications; and won over the second by conjuring up the disorders which would inevitably attend a simultaneous transfer of both the legislative and executive powers in 1852.

The inoffensive Ministry proved an ideal front for the plot. The real movers remained in the background: Morny, a consummate politician with all the daring of a gambler; Saint-Arnaud, as courageous as he was unscrupulous, a man whose hero's death rather than his life would have caught the attention of Plutarch; Persigny, a fanatically devoted friend, but demanding, difficult, and unpredictable, as only devotion itself sometimes can be; and Maupas, whose talents were somewhat unequal to such a risky undertaking. They were all there, silent and still like soldiers awaiting the signal to attack. At the last minute the Prince wavered. Did he have qualms? There is no denying his fondness for intrigue. Yet, at once obstinate and indolent by nature, he liked to ruminate, and he would have preferred to continue dreaming about a successful coup. However, time was running out. Persigny gave him a good shove, while Morny, his brother, gently led him by the hand. Louis Bonaparte's victory was complete: dictatorship today, tomorrow the Empire.

The need for deviousness was gone. Yet the habit had been formed and the successful Sovereign continued to intrigue even as the ill-starred pretender once had. Was it a case of congenital insincerity? It was rather the natural bent of a mind too complicated to grasp simple, clear-cut things. It was perhaps due to the pleasure which a dilettante derives from doing things the hard way. This suspicious nature was not free from a measure of naiveté. The same man, who rejected common sense solutions as vulgar, could show a blind faith in his empirical conclusions. He was as often as not the victim of his own suspicions. Even at the height of power, he remained aloof not only from his family—which is easy enough to understand, but from his friends, and his most faithful servants. While carrying out what they conceived to be the proper functions of their office, his most loyal ministers could never be sure that they had not been hoaxed. Few cabinet meetings were held, and those only for the form. He much preferred private talks with three or four advisers. Or, better yet, he liked to engage in long solitary meditations during which he could mull over his ideas, and review the pros and cons of a given project until his own mind was divided against itself. That, after all, was but another way of conspiring.

Thus, although his decisions were usually the product of long deliberations, they were unexpected and often gave the impression of having been reached on the spur of the moment.

This disconcerting manner of governing manifested itself on three occasions—not to mention many others. In 1860, the Treaty of Commerce, which was to have such profound effects on the French economy, was secretly drafted and negotiated in plotlike fashion. In 1866, the nefarious treaty allying Prussia and Italy was concluded under the auspices of the Emperor, acting as the sole representative of France. Finally, we have it from Empress Eugénie herself that, in July, 1870, the fateful decision to demand the guarantee which led inexorably to war was taken, not at a cabinet meeting, but during a conversation between the Emperor, the Empress, and M. de Gramont.

No man was ever more secretive than this prince; no man ever formulated his doctrines with more perseverence. He was anything but an improvisator. In his early writings one can find, in embryo, all the basic concepts which he was later to use as guidelines.

The first tenet in his credo was popular sovereignty. Although the nation might delegate its powers, it reserved the ultimate and superior right to reclaim the authority it had granted as a trusteeship. Bonaparte proclaimed this doctrine at the age of twenty-four, and he was to reassert it in his hour of triumph. This recognition of the people's rights was a kind of homage paid by the head of state to another, even more exalted sovereign.

However, popular sovereignty and hereditary rights are mutually exclusive. In the *Rêveries,* Louis Bonaparte, who prided himself on his logic, did not dare to affirm the doctrine of hereditary succession. The people's consent would be needed at the beginning of each new reign. Should it be withheld, the Chambers would designate a new Emperor. He did not, however, hold on to this line of thinking for very long. Indeed, he next sought to endow the ruler with so much prestige that the people, as if hypnotized, would readily place their destinies in his hands and those of his successors. This done, the people would no longer care to exercise what would gradually become a dormant and nominal claim to sovereignty. This, at least, was the theme developed in the *Idées napoléoniennes,* published at London in 1839. The *Idées* were not in direct contradiction to the *Rêveries;* but the second work represented a definite attempt to fuse all things in the image of the Great Emperor, who was pictured as a superman and a demigod. With Napoleon I, a new order had been born. From him his heirs derived a natural vocation to reign. It amounted to a substitution of Napoleonic right for Divine right—but under the cover of popular sovereignty. How then could the people exercise its will under such a system? The more the Prince realized the difficulty of finding a practicable answer, the louder he proclaimed the principle of popular sovereignty. The new doctrines had been enunciated by the time of the death of the Duke of Reichstadt. As soon as he became the head of his House, Louis-Napoleon laid claim to all the privileges, and assumed all the responsibilities of his position. He began playing the role of pretender with such assurance that he gave the impression of being as imbued with the righteousness of his cause as Louis XVIII once had been with his. Nothing could shake his faith. He remained unaffected by poverty, exile, and obscurity. Neither the failure of two attempted coups, nor the scorn or indifference of public opinion, or a sentence to life imprisonment could even momentarily dim an incurable optimism. Alone to believe in his star, he closed his eyes to realities, and stumbled forward to keep his rendezvous with destiny like a sleepwalker or a man possessed. The heir of the Bonapartes was so careful to identify himself with the glory surrounding his name, that this incredible infatuation did not prove harmful in the least!

Having made up his own horoscope, he tailored his concepts to it. He always took a broad view of things. France occupied too small a place in the overall world picture to attract his whole attention. He intended to remap Europe while governing France. His ideas were as daring as his uncle's deeds. In Switzerland, in England, and especially at the fortress of Ham, in exile as in prison, he filled long pages, tiring by their unrelieved solemnity, but in which can be found all the plans of the future Emperor. Children, when they first begin to study geography, are always struck by the odd shapes of the various states. Their young and logical minds fail to grasp the part played by time, treaties, and the need to shorten or avoid wars in determining what may first appear as a haphazard delimitation of territories. With the daring of innocence, they long for a world built with the square blocks of their earlier games. Louis Bonaparte had similar longings. He also played with blocks (what better way to while away the days at Ham?); a harmless enough pastime so long as it does not proceed beyond the level of a game. He was especially attracted by large-scale political entities like the United States and Russia. Much of Europe, parcelled as it was, badly needed to be consolidated. In his eagerness to rebuild, even at France's door, he sometimes forgot France herself. Napoleon I had already reduced the number of German states. But many more alterations would have to be made before the map of Germany became a symmetric and pleasing sight. Italy, with its comic opera principalities, was in equal need of reorganization. No less urgent, but of a different nature, was the task of liberating the subject peoples of the Austrian Empire. Awed by his own sacred formulas, the Prince came to think of himself not so much as a reformer, but rather as an apostle.

The right of a people to choose its own government was a corollary of the principle of popular sovereignty, the basic tenet in his credo. Another corollary, respect for natural frontiers, turned into a holy crusade any attempt to remap Europe along lines predetermined by nature. Finally, the principle of national self-determination, a third corollary, entailed the emancipation of subject peoples. Popular sovereignty, natural frontiers, and national self-determination were the three main principles which made up Louis Bonaparte's political philosophy from the very start. The seeds were sown; the fruits would ripen someday. . . .

One can properly begin an evaluation of Napoleon III's impact on French History by saying that he was the very opposite of the Bourbons. Although they had ruled wisely more often than not, the latter had made themselves unpopular at home by their repeated tactlessness. In foreign affairs, however, they had always instinctively understood the real and long-range interests of France. France had gradually been built as the result of their painstaking labors. Soldiers, diplomats, the quiet but efficient clerks of the Ministry of Foreign Affairs—all had made their contributions to the common task. The reverse is true of Napoleon III. At home, no ruler was more sensitive to the longings of public opinion. By adapting his policy to them, sometimes even by anticipating them, he was able to satisfy the nation. In foreign policy, misguided generosity, illusions, and ignorance caused him to lose sight of the national interest to an extent equally unparalleled in our history.

The electorate's continued loyalty to Napoleon III is one of the most notable features of his reign. The people, who had adopted the Prince at the beginning of his career, never refused to give him a vote of confidence. The nation elected him in 1848, sanctioned the coup d'état, and acclaimed the advent of the Second Empire. There were four legislative elections (in 1852, 1857, 1863, 1869), and each time the nation's will to keep him on the throne was clearly asserted—although with varying majorities. Even when the signs of a declining fortune became obvious, the votes did not reflect the nation's misgivings. Almost on the eve of the regime's downfall, the results of the plebiscite, at once triumphant and funereal, revealed that the thirst for stability had not yet been offset by this loss of confidence.

This stubborn attachment can be explained by the prestige of the name of Napoleon; a name so great that it could bear the brunt of repeated mistakes without losing its magic. It can be explained, at least in the agrarian areas, by sustained prosperity. It can be explained by the attraction of a regime incarnating equality, glory, and a disciplined revolution; a regime generating at once a sense of security and a feeling of emancipation. Finally, the personal qualities of the Sovereign were an important factor. Good, benevolent, kind-hearted, high-minded, generous, prompt to express his gratitude for services rendered, he maintained a close rapport with his people. Moreover, as a consummate stage manager and producer, he knew the full value of glorious spectacles, dramatic disclosures, and inspiring gestures. The changes of scenery came so fast under the Second Empire than one had no time to be bored. It might be added that the incorporating of the principle of popular sovereignty in the constitution was a master stroke. For the people, even while bowing before stringent laws, found consolation in the thought that its master was, after all, the popularly chosen leader of an orderly democracy. . . .

In my old age, I have not been able to resist the temptation of reassessing this man, the history of whose reign I once wrote. He was indeed nefarious. But no sooner have I written this, than I would like to soften the harshness of the judgment; for he was also good and, at times, enlightened. Of Napoleon III, Émile de Girardin once said: "Were we still living in the days when one attached labels to the names of princes, we would call him 'Napoleon the Well-Meaning.' " This epithet aptly sums up this benevolent, quixotic, weak, and self-indulgent man. When one remembers his intense desire to do good, one is tempted to rank him among those men of good will to whom the Scriptures promise peace on earth and everlasting life in the next world. I cannot help thinking, however, that the celestial spirits, who announced this divine message on Christmas night, would have been dismayed to discover that so much good will could create such confusion. Frightened by this chaos, they would not have lingered on earth, but promptly returned to the heavens where true peace reigns.

A. F. Thompson
FROM RESTORATION TO REPUBLIC

A Fellow of Wadham College and University Lecturer in Modern History at Oxford University, A. F. Thompson's main interests lie in English and French history in the 19th and 20th centuries. Although Thompson (b. 1920) is objective in his attempt to present the Second Empire in its historical context, his labelling Napoleon III a "Chekovian romantic" echoes the appellations of earlier critics. Since A. F. Thompson is a colleague and a contemporary of Theodore Zeldin at Oxford, the divergence in their views is symptomatic of the lingering debate over the Second Empire.

After June, in the second phase of the Second Republic, there was little doubt who had to be satisfied. Monarchy was dead, and the masses cowed; terms could now be made to provide for those who really mattered. If a republic was unavoidable, it must be conservative in form; as far as was feasible restricted in electoral basis; and with a strong executive, to make the world safe for the common man of property. A substitute was required which might fulfill the expectations of constitutional monarchy in 1830, without recourse to kings. But, despite the elimination of alternatives, the

From A. F. Thompson, "From Restoration to Republic," in J. M. Wallace-Hadrill and J. McManners, eds., *France: Government and Society* (London, 1957). Reprinted by permission of the author and Methuen & Co. Ltd.

idea of a republic remained repugnant to many Frenchmen; and traditional doubts and half-formulated fears had been given force by events in Paris before the views of right-thinking men were asserted by Cavaignac. The origins of the Second Republic, tainted by "socialism" and the prominence of the poor, would have made its reformation difficult enough for the new masters had they made no mistakes. To promote the election of Louis-Napoleon as first President was to be too clever by half. They knew they faced a heavy task, and hoped to bring a great name to their assistance in the choice of a man of straw. But, in uneasy circumstances where confidence is lacking, it is dangerous to tamper with explosive myths. An elected President, given real power and a wide popular appeal, might outmaneuver and destroy those who had intended to employ him for their own secure establishment. For all their careful calculations, the liberal intellectuals, still talking and scheming, were soon driven from the scene by what Marx aptly called "the eighteenth Brumaire of Louis-Napoleon," less by force than by a legend.

Over the past generation a Bonapartist myth had been gradually built up. There were always mourners anxious to commemorate, embellish, and inflate the achievements of the great Emperor. In and after 1848, the legend, based upon a solid foundation of fact, was found to possess an irresistible attraction, and the snags of empire were forgotten. Among the difficulties of making the republic viable and respectable, there appeared another solution, urged upon a hesitant but receptive France by the mystical self-confidence of Louis-Napoleon. Greatness and stability might be restored with the Empire; and, after all, who had done most to create what bourgeois and peasant wanted to preserve and cherish? Louis-Philippe had failed in his task, and one's support was withheld; then his immediate heirs came to seem as bad as Charles X, if not worse in their very different way. Even after June, could the Republic ever be trusted? Hard as the Thiers and Tocquevilles struggled, they were trapped by the past; by their own constitution-making and over-smart politics; and by the adroit exploitation of a perfect opportunity by his uncle's nephew.

Louis-Napoleon as President displayed an ostentatious concern for the defense of interests he rightly identified as vital, accumulating much credit. What was wanted, he believed, was firm administration, resting upon a semblance of representative government, and conducted with a suitable panache and in the hope of glory. The latter was especially important if the loyalty of the Army was to be secured for the coup d'état. In fact, those who might have erected the barricades were exiled, cowed, or saw nothing to defend; while comfortable scholars do not fight in the streets. Personified and in action, the legend found no opposition worth the name from men who retired with what grace they could muster, confidently and indeed accurately predicting disaster.

Resounding approval of this easy victory came through one legacy of 1848, universal suffrage, which had brought the peasant fully into politics, visibly at the side of the bourgeois. *"Le suffrage universel finit toujours par discerner et récompenser ses véritables amis,"* said the optimistic Gambetta. Whatever might happen in the long run, Louis-Napoleon's experience taught conservatives a lesson concerning the initial results of such a change which was not lost upon either Bismarck or Disraeli. In Namier's phrase, demagogic despotism is "the desperate shift of communities broken from their moorings"; and in the drifting, dissatisfied France of 1852 the promise of bread and circuses was well-timed. For a while at least, Church, peasant, businessman and soldier could all be bribed to support a retrial of the one previous system not recently discredited. Indeed, little bribery was needed: most Frenchmen surrendered happily to the tyranny of the plausible myth, abandoning liberty and the freedom to choose their masters.

The Second Empire often appears as a feeble echo of its great predecessor. That truly weak man, Napoleon III, was a derivative, conjuring up strength from the legend which carried him to power. In his policies, at home and abroad, aping of the original is obvious time and time again. Yet he was something more than a mere plagiarist, and even careful copying might ensure a modicum of success. From the start the regime had its enemies; later, notably through the twists and turns of a doctrinaire foreign policy incompetently executed, it acquired more. But there were many who did well, and dramatically well, out of this latest experiment. Rigged as they were, the plebiscites of 1870 show a broad measure of continuing support; while the void after Sedan, and the difficulty of finding a replacement, are notorious. The available evidence suggests that the revived Empire provided real benefits on a considerable scale; and, above all, that it proved the system which least displeased most Frenchmen. Napoleon III destroyed his own creation: he was not overthrown, any more than the Third Republic in 1940, by critics turned revolutionaries, as were the regimes of 1815, 1830, and 1848. This Chekhovian romantic could produce results, and as master of the most politically "mature" nation in Europe. There had been much to enjoy; when he fell to the Germans, there was much to regret.

Especially in the economic sphere, success was due to good luck as well as good management. In the nineteenth century, France never experienced an industrial revolution comparable to those in England or Germany. At the end of the century it remained largely what it had been in 1815; the country of localized, small-scale industrial development, tending to be antiquated if highly skilled in its methods, and more concerned with secondary than primary production. Still preponderantly an agrarian economy, its characteristic figures were those of the property-owning peasant, his cultivation as conservative as his outlook, and the bourgeois merchant, shopkeeper, small master, and professional man, only in Paris and a few of the greatest towns far from the land and the psychology of the petty rural proprietor. Under the July Monarchy, with its high tariffs and concern for the businessmen and farmers of Balzac and Flaubert, the difficulties of the postwar period diminished, and the trend was generally if patchily upward. Increased prosperity at some levels and in certain groups did not necessarily imply a reflection elsewhere, as the condition of the urban working class before 1848 demonstrated. Nevertheless, the peasant and the bourgeois were better off by the time of the coup d'état than they had been a generation earlier, with more to protect or lose. Improvements in technique in well-established trades, enhanced efficiency in financial organization and the extension of communications, combined with a slow growth of population and a favorable fiscal policy, promised further gains. This promise was not disappointed; and it seems certain that the Second Empire was a period of increased general prosperity, as it was undoubtedly one of considerable economic innovation.

How far the régime itself contributed to this development is not yet clear. Napoleon III set the fashion for dictators in promoting public works, and the largesse was widely distributed. His motives might be mixed: the streets of Paris had to be rendered unsafe for barricades, and avenues cleared for the whiff of grapeshot. However,

Haussmann's truly imperial planning meant money in the contractor's pocket and wages for the workingman. Here was a more effective substitute for the National Workshops, producing visible and magnificent results. Of more general importance was the encouragement of easier credit, and more adventurous banking, calculated to assist and please the commercial and industrial entrepreneur; and, while reactions here might be more variable, notably to the Cobden Treaty, fiscal policy was designed to cater for the friends of the system. Most of all, perhaps, the state played a significant part in the greatest and most beneficial change of these years, the improvement of communications by road, rail, and water, which tapped the potentialities of a well-established economy without revolutionizing it. Here indeed were echoes of the First Empire.

Whatever the true explanation, Napoleon III got the praise for changes when they were good, as he got the blame when they were not. There is little doubt where the balance lay. Even among the urban workers, with whom earlier regimes had so notably failed, life improved. The agitations of the sixties for improved status, especially for the unions, were those of men more concerned with conditions of work than with politics—which, in the French context, is to say a great deal. However, the greatest gains were elsewhere, to the bourgeoisie and, above all, to the peasantry. For the latter a vastly better standard of living began to emerge, which was to deepen further an innate conservatism and to prove so important under the Third Republic. Materially, the Second Empire served well those whose dominant position in French society the First had done so much to determine; and from his investments, so fortunate as well as so well-placed, Napoleon III drew a handsome political dividend. Moreover, the task of his enemies was increased, as their numbers and vehemence were reduced, by a prosperity for which government could fairly claim some credit.

Nevertheless, the weaknesses of the revived Empire are obvious. Like the great Napoleon, a lesser man, under less propitious circumstances for his country and himself, had to face and overcome all the dangers which beset the usurping despot, especially when he appeals to "the people" for survival without an efficient army or an effective secret police. The possibility of serious external failure, invariably disastrous, was always present after 1859; while at home the autocrat, particularly when he is successful enough to have the problem of securing a succession, makes a multiplicity of enemies, not least through rigidity and exclusion, the stigmata of an aging dictatorship. To Napoleon III the first of these dangers, catastrophe in foreign policy, came with a vengeance; but in dealing with the second, it is less clear that he failed.

The "Liberal Empire" presents a fascinating problem: how far can autocracy modify itself and placate its critics without losing control? To assert that the last of the Bonapartes was defeated by this difficulty would be rash. Modification under pressure, before it became too strong for comfort, was his strategy from 1860; as indeed he had promised earlier, remembering the underlying weakness of his uncle even at the height of his vast powers. Those who felt they had extorted concessions thought often enough of alternatives, but the system managed to contain them; and after 1869 it is doubtful whether the most dangerous opponents had not been bought off. Moreover, beyond the reconciliation, precarious perhaps, of men like Thiers and Ollivier, the plebiscites suggested a firm basis of support. What were such squibs as the Belleville program compared with this? In 1870 few substantial citizens were seeking more than amendment of the régime. Sedan forced them to do so, and they found the search exceedingly difficult. In the eyes of many Frenchmen, Napoleon III had lived up to his own precept: *"un gouvernement n'est donc pas un ulcère nécessaire, mais c'est plutôt le moteur bienfaisant de tout organisme social."* What could take his place?

Marcel Blanchard

NAPOLEON III: AIMS, ACHIEVEMENTS, AND FAILURES

Marcel Blanchard, a former professor at the Faculté des Lettres of the University of Paris, was endowed with a rare gift for synthesis. His Histoire du Second Empire, first published in 1950, was awarded the Prix Auguste-Gérard by the Académie des Sciences Morales et Politiques. Abreast of the latest scholarship, moderate in tone, balanced in its judgments, this slim volume is one of the best short introductions to the study of the Second Empire. In the excerpt below, Blanchard reviews the achievements and failures of the reign in the light of Napoleon III's self-assigned goals.

The Emperor, who was at most of average intelligence, had observed much and acquired a broad if superficial and uneven understanding of many things. To be sure, he had tenaciously sought power for all its immediate advantages. Yet, he had also looked ahead and formulated some long range goals. If he was without a detailed, carefully worked-out program, he had some definite ideas as to what he hoped to accomplish.

First and foremost, he intended to promote the material welfare of the French people. He had witnessed the sudden industrial upsurge of Great Britain and perceived the series of innovations which had brought about this transformation. From his exile, he had viewed France as a large and powerful country, rich and well-endowed with natural resources, which was falling behind because of poor administration. Thus he deemed that, as a starting point, the modernization of the French economy should be accelerated. Agriculture must be safeguarded and made more productive, the reclamation of French soil completed, and the rural population—all too often underfed and in dire straits—transformed into a well-to-do peasantry. Industrial growth must be encouraged in all of its various facets. The country must be linked by the nation-wide extension of the railroad network begun under the July Monarchy, and the construction of a connecting highway system. Inland waterways must be extended and connected with open water ports.

From Marcel Blanchard, *Le Second Empire* (2nd ed.; Paris, 1956). Reprinted by permission of Librairie Armand Colin. Editor's translation.

Ancient towns must be made into new, spacious, modern, and comfortable cities. Finally, French trade must be spurred throughout the Mediterranean world and beyond. In brief, he sought to bring up to new heights the material and moral standards of the masses. Thus would he establish a solid base for the preponderant role which he wished France to play in world affairs. This remained one of his cardinal aims. He never renounced it, and recalled it with moving and ultimate sincerity during the last days of exile and decrepitude.

With the same singleness of purpose, he was to pursue a second, perhaps less apparent goal: the repudiation of those treaties of 1815 which stood as symbols of the downfall of his dynasty and the decline of France. He sought to clear the continent from the lingering aura of the anti-French coalition, and to substitute a new atmosphere stemming from the remapping of Europe (into individual states or federations?) through the fulfillment of national aspirations. Needless to say, France would take the lead in, and derive profit from this reorganization. Because of her strategic position and intensified material progress, she would bring the new political units within her orbit. The harsh military dominance of yesteryears would be replaced by a kind of pacific and humanitarian supremacy over a Europe fascinated in spite of herself by the memorial of Saint-Helena.

The restoration of the Empire would prove the means to these ends. But, and that was the third point in his program, the Emperor would derive his powers from the sovereign people. Firmly convinced in the validity of his doctrines, he assumed a priori the impossibility of a divorce between the Emperor and the people. How could Frenchmen fail to answer joyously his call to win the fight against poverty at home, and to initiate spectacular changes abroad from which France would gain both profit and honor? Between the Emperor and the people he would leave no vacuum where the parasitic parliamentarians might find refuge. While he was eventually to consent to the creation of an elective Legislative Body, its mandate was highly diffused, and he reserved the right to influence its make-up. At most, the elections to the Legislative Body would serve as a double-check on the results of the periodic plebiscites. Never would they be allowed to vitiate the expressed will of the nation.

Although he had seen the "machine" system at work in America, he did not favor partisan politics any more than English parliamentarism. From the Napoleonic myth, he had retained the concept of a national mission, above and beyond parties and party organizations. To present the parties as harmful factions and their standing committees as the ever mobilized forces of anarchy; to offer himself as the sole, personal, and responsible leader, as the incarnation of a revived government authority: that, in the final analysis, was his fundamental pretension. Napoleon's design, doubtless naive but certainly sincere, was to eliminate the parties, to rally all their assimilable elements behind a great, constructive policy of public weal; and, if not to keep the remnants outside the pale of the French community, at least to reduce the irreconcilables either to inoffensive sulk or powerless hatred. He was to proclaim his faithfulness to this goal to the very end.

What support could the Emperor initially count on for such risky undertakings? Could he hope to find and select some truly faithful collaborators? Would the Notables willingly give up their traditional control of the state to become the disciplined cadres of the great enterprise? Would they merely lend him their temporary assistance? Or, for that matter, would they abstain and stand ready to regain the upper hand at the earliest opportunity? And would this man of Saint-Simonian leanings, who longed to be loved in his own right, accept the almost contemptuous promise of so many Catholic legitimists, not of personal devotion, but of support for those of his policies in defense of religion, the family, property, and authority? Above all, could he count on the passive acceptance of the democrats? Would public opinion lose its interest in politics, place its destinies in the hands of the Emperor, and give him a perennially renewed vote of confidence? Could the elected savior of the rural population and the Party of Order avoid either the corruption of unlimited power, or surrendering to the old centralized bureaucracy?

These questions are all the more valid because Napoleon III did not operate according to any strict methods. This is not to say that he was without application. Quite the contrary, he studied, or caused to be studied, all problems brought to his attention. All those who worked with him invariably praised his affability, his careful consideration of objections, and his desire to be kept informed. If he was apt to take sudden initiatives, they were the result of mature deliberation. But he especially lacked a proper training. Neither as a lawyer, nor as a technician had he ever learned to study a dossier. And he never seems to have grasped the practical implications of his decisions. Moreover, from his past as a conspirator, Napoleon III had retained a fondness for devious means of information, personal contacts, and mysterious interviews. He might have governed through the bureaucracy. One can easily imagine the Emperor at the apex, in full control of the functionaries, constantly urging them to greater action and efficiency, implacably removing the lazy and the incapable. He soon realized, however, that even with such a powerful instrument as the Constitution of 1852, the deadweight of the centralized bureaucracy was a strong obstacle to any really meaningful innovation. Thus, in many cases, he became the prisoner of the machinery of government.

[As we have seen] Napoleon had a threefold objective when he assumed absolute power: the inducement of political lethargy through the elimination of the parties; the promotion of prosperity and well-being through economic growth; and the remapping of Europe through the revision of the Treaties of Vienna. What had been accomplished toward the realization of these goals by the time of the regime's downfall? What can be entered on the credit and debit sides of the ledger?

On the economic plane, and it may be dealt with first because there is no doubt as to the answer, the verdict is complete success. To be sure, one might criticize the financial methods, underline the dishonesty of certain officials, regret the sacrifice of, or the lesser consideration given to, certain interest groups, and accentuate some gaps and shadows in the overall picture. But the prodigious commercial expansion, the rapid pace of industrialization, the extension of the railroad network, the thorough reorganization of the banking system—all represent great achievements. To these must be added the rebuilding of Paris. In the area of economics, the Second Empire was certainly the most startling success in French history.

On the plane of domestic policies, one is tempted to render a verdict of total failure. During the early years of his dictatorship, Louis-Napoleon tried to remove from public life both the Marianne and the Rue de Poitiers, the Montagnards and the Burgraves. Yet,

FIGURES 5 and 6. This study in contrasts is symptomatic of the difficulties confronting the historian who seeks to identify the "real" Napoleon III. He certainly was not endowed with the royal bearing depicted in the official portrait; nor was he by any means "The End of the Legend." (*Photo. Bibl. nat. Paris*)

he was forced to come to terms with the latter as early as 1860, and he was eventually overthrown by the former. He had wanted to eradicate partisanship and to dissolve the parties. Actually, the parties absorbed his dictatorship long before partisans swept out his regime.

Are we to conclude, then, that nothing of long range importance occurred on the home front from December 2nd to Sedan? That these were dead years? That these are interpolated pages which could be removed without in any way altering the pattern of French politics? Under no circumstances could one presume to ignore eighteen years of history. One must indeed probe the matter further. The perspective of time behooves us to be at once less partial and more perspicacious.

If universal suffrage be the inevitable mode of expression of popular sovereignty, the Second Empire, in spite of the system of official candidacies, was an apprenticeship, and a decisive moment in the democratic evolution of the country. It was especially influential in the political formation of the French peasantry. Among those observers who have analyzed rural Bonapartism, the most qualified have pointed out that during the last years of the 19th century, after some thirty years of Republic, large segments of the rural population suddenly passed from an authentic Bonapartism to an equally authentic radicalism. This was an extremely significant development. The Second Empire worked against the interests of the Notables. No one knew it better than those members of the Third Party who fought so hard against the Emperor's personal power. And this permits the suggestion of a thesis which the pensioners of December 2d would have dismissed as sacrilegious: in the decisive battle which is the key to an understanding of well-nigh a half-century of Republic (1877–1914), i.e., the laborious, bitter, and inexorable elimination of the traditional Notables by the democracy of "Committees" and "Small Interest," it is entirely plausible that, in the final analysis, the latter were able to crush their opponents and consolidate the hegemony of caciques of an entirely different stamp because of the legacy of the Second Empire.

The foreign policy of the Second Empire led to military disaster and territorial loss. A clear-cut pronouncement of failure might thus be in order. Here also, however, it is worthwhile to venture beyond the beaten path. One might ponder, for instance, whether this failure was not due to precarious means rather than erroneous ends. Against the wishes of the majority of informed French public opinion and the advice of the technicians and professionals, the Emperor sought to upset the European status quo. But he never clearly assessed the prerequisites of success. More precisely, he lacked the courage to impose the necessary sacrifices on the country—even less on the privileged classes than on the masses. Thus he was never able to build up a military establishment commensurate to his continental policies. He was a gambler who overplayed a weak hand. This leads one to wonder whether he ever really understood the basic requirements of French foreign policy.

The mastery of the continent, his innermost aim, was difficult to reconcile with the movement toward national self-determination which he sought to initiate and sponsor. He dominated Europe only for a brief moment, from the Congress of Paris to Solferino at the very most. But we may be allowed to believe that even while helping the process of unification, or at least maintaining a benevolent neutrality, he might still have won some compensations for France had he avoided the disastrous Mexican embroglio and concentrated his energies on Mediterranean and colonial expansion. In fact, there were some splendid achievements in that direction: the emergence of a French sphere of influence in Turkey; the establishment of such a foothold in the Levant that we were to remain the quasi-masters of the area until 1914; the opening of Suez and the transformation of Alexandria into a second Marseille; the penetration of Tunisia and the supervision of Morocco. To think that the same Wimpfen, who fought at Sedan in 1870, had just come home from an expedition to the Upper Guir! We would not be able to return to that region until 1908. Similar opportunities presented themselves in China and Indochina. Had it not been for the Hohenzollern affair, we could have avenged and taken advantage of the massacre of French nationals at Tientsin, June, 1870. All this leads one to conclude, with reasonable confidence, that the Emperor's greatest error was to repeat the mistake of Louis XV by giving priority to continental politics, at the very moment when the spread of European dominance over the globe was gathering new momentum.

In the final analysis, as against Napoleon III, it was Prévost-

Paradol who was right in pointing to a new French Africa, and we might add to a vast overseas empire, as the right avenues toward the fulfillment of French *grandeur*.

James Matthew Thompson
THE HAMLET OF FRENCH HISTORY

James Matthew Thompson (1878–1956), an Oxford scholar, enjoyed a long and prolific career. His last book, Louis-Napoleon and the Second Empire, *published shortly before his death, came as a natural sequel to his previous studies on the Revolution of 1789 and the First Empire. This "trilogy" has assured Mr. Thompson of a lasting reputation in the field. The author's refusal to accept the traditional lines of demarcation of the Second Empire, and his obvious reluctance to pass a final judgment on Napoleon III will serve as a final reminder that the last word has yet to be written on the man and his reign.*

Historians like to divide their subject into definite periods by significant dates. The Empire which began in December 1852 is commonly held to have reached a first peak of success at the Peace of Paris in March, 1856, and a second at the Treaty of Zürich in November, 1859, then to have entered into a decline, leading to the crisis of Sadowa in July, 1866, and the catastrophe of Sedan in September, 1870. These divisions may be accepted. But how do they link up with the internal development of the Empire? This is commonly divided into two periods—the Authoritarian Empire, 1852–1859, and the Liberal Empire, 1860–69. This partition is justified by the Liberal concessions made in November, 1860, November, 1861, and January, 1867; but it gives too little significance to the elections in June, 1857, May, 1863, and May, 1869—political barometer readings of the state of the national atmosphere—and it does not bring out the influence of such events as the Orsini plot (January, 1858), the Anglo-French commercial treaty (January, 1860), the Polish insurrection

Reprinted by permission of Farrar, Straus & Giroux, and Basil Blackwell & Mott Ltd., from *Louis-Napoleon and the Second Empire* by J. M. Thompson, copyright 1955 by J. M. Thompson.

(January, 1863), or the death of Morny (March, 1865) upon the political situation. In fact, the character of the Empire was changing all the time: there was no one moment at which authoritarianism ended and liberalism began: Louis himself had always intended his regime to conform throughout to a pre-fixed pattern—*la suite dans les idées napoléoniennes.* That it failed to do so was his tragedy. Why it failed to do so—how far through his own failings, how far from circumstances outside his control—has to be inquired.

The pattern which Louis imagined himself to be imposing upon the country was a misinterpretation of the First Empire in the light of 1815—the year whose experiences had, even in his mother's mind, nearly effaced all that went before. He supposed, as Napoleon himself had almost come to believe at St. Helena, that the *acte additionnel* was not a temporary concession to win the support of the Liberals for an attempt to renew the dictatorship, but a step in the natural development of that dictatorship into a constitutional monarchy. Authoritarianism was to give way to Liberalism. Liberty was to crown the edifice of the Empire. This misreading of Napoleon's real mind was conscious and deliberate; for Louis well knew that little more would have been heard of the *acte additionnel* if Napoleon had won at Waterloo. He now found himself faced by much the same dilemma. The unpopularity of the July Monarchy, the Parisian fear of Red Revolution, and the power of the name Napoleon amongst the mass of the people all pointed towards a Second Empire rather than another constitutional monarchy. It would have required a clearer conviction and a stronger will than Louis ever possessed to initiate at once in 1852 the transition from despotism to liberalism, from force to freedom, which he professed as part of the Napoleonic idea. He found that the authoritarian Empire *worked;* and he set about devising ways of making its authority acceptable, putting off the difficult day when, whether acceptable or not, it was ex hypothesi to be liberalized. This interim policy would satisfy the army with foreign adventures, placate the Church by garrisoning Rome, win bourgeois support by an industrial drive and a reduction of tariffs, conciliate Parisian opposition by "clearing the slums" and creating new building sites, and raise the whole public morale by showy fêtes, expensive court functions, and international expositions.

But the weakness of an interim policy is that it deals with the surface symptoms of disease, not with its root causes. It was impossible to indulge the army in military adventures without rousing the hostility of the European powers. Louis' Italian policy after 1859 was no longer acceptable to his Catholic supporters, who knew that he would take the first opportunity to leave the Pope to his fate. It was difficult to favor "big business" and the factory-owners without ignoring the claims of the workers, and playing into the hands of socialist agitators. The "Haussmannizing" of Paris created those housing difficulties and financial scandals with which Zola's *La Curée* shocked the next generation—the generation that had to pay for the rebuilding of the capital. Fêtes and festivities were patronized by foreigners or nouveaux riches, whilst the old aristocracy stood aloof: court extravagance reminded people more of the Bourbon Monarchy than of the Napoleonic Empire. The Exposition of 1855 compared poorly with the Great Exhibition of 1851; that of 1867 was overshadowed by the ill omens of Sadowa and Querétaro.

Already, in the early years of the Second Empire, its weaknesses began to appear, and opposition to be organized. There were things which even a "Man of Destiny" could not do; persons whom even Louis' charm and kindness—weapons so unlike those of his great predecessor—could not conciliate. The cloak of despotism had never fitted the shoulders of a visionary humanitarian, a friend of the outlawed and the oppressed. Louis' policy, like his mind, was divided between his mission and his career, his schemes for the betterment of France and Europe and the security of the position which would enable him to carry them out. The Empire, he thought, must be at once repressive and progressive. It must use all the powers that the panic and proscription of 1848–51 had put into his hands to maintain order; and it must exploit all the opportunities offered by an expanding world-market to the most thrifty and hard-working people in Western Europe. By one way or another every class in the community must be kept contented and cooperative. This was indeed a Bourbon idea: Louis XIV would have understood it, Colbert would have exploited it. It was also a Napoleonic idea: this part of the *Idées napoléoniennes* was not legendary, but true to fact. Unhappily Louis was neither a *Grand Monarque* nor a *Napoléon le Grand;* France had grown fifty years older since Brumaire; and the Second Empire could only be, like most sequels, something of an anti-climax. Louis' "enlightened despotism" came a century too late in European history.

Yet it could all be looked at in another way. Louis was a man of vision, surrounded by commonplace minds: a man with a mission amongst compromisers and careerists; a man of mystery whom no one rightly understood. His visions were distorted into programs, his mission faded away into diplomatic agreements, his mystery was made the excuse for hesitations and mistakes. Yet something in him remained unspoiled, unpublicized—an integrity of mind, a generous purpose of well-doing, which put to shame the policy he was driven to by circumstances and associates. He was a man to be pitied more than to be blamed.

. . . Now that I have come to the end of the life, I am not sure how to sum it up. To write a man's life is not to make a list of all he did, year by year, from his birth to his death, as though each act had the same worth. It is to paint a work of art, in which the light and shade fall where they should, if the man is to look as God and the world made him. His mind was his own before birth; what he has done is still marked on his face when he is dead. Who can say past doubt that while he lived he was to be blamed, or that when he died he had failed?

This was a life ruled from first to last by a great name; a life hitched to a star; a life in which fate—now kind, now hard—seemed to hold the strings and to guide the moves. What can I say of it all, but that here he took the right turn, and there the wrong; that this thought of his seems to have been true to his best self, and this not; that he had his eyes fixed on a goal, but could not find the way to reach it? For I think that at the back of all his twists and turns, all his ups and downs, he held close in his mind and warm in his heart the will to be great and the wish to do good; and that he must be judged, if at all, by the ends he tried to win more than by the means he took to win them: by the France of *l'ordre* and *la gloire* which he hoped to build up out of the heap of stones fate put at his feet; by all he risked and dared so that he might set free the land of his first fame; by the new Rome that he thought—but not as the Pope thought—might rise out of the old; by the seeds of fresh life he would have sown in the far east and west and south; by the rights of race and tongue that he wished to make safe for all the world; yes, and—since he won more trust as a man than as a prince—by the love of his friends, the faith he shared with the crowd, and the care he showed for the poor. By these he should be judged, not by the wrong ways in which, now and then, he tried to win his ends.

Yet he was a man too small for the great things he set out to do; too prone to be led by weak or bad friends; too quick to take dreams for facts; one who walked in his sleep, and woke too late to save a fall. And so I have been led to put at the head of each scene of his life some lines from the play in which a brave and wise young prince, called to mend a deep wrong done to his house, and born to set right a world that is out of joint, finds that the task is too much for him, and that he has not the strength to make his dreams come true.

V EPILOGUE

René Rémond
BONAPARTISM AND GAULLISM

René Rémond (b. 1918), who attended the Ecole Normale Supérieure *and earned his* Doctorat d'Etat *at the University of Paris, ranks among the keenest and most prolific students of modern French history. His colleagues in the field can only hope that the administrative duties he assumed in 1971, as President of the University of Paris X (Nanterre), will not overly interfere with his scholarly pursuits. The excerpt below is taken from* La Droite en France, *one of his most stimulating works.*

It always is profitable to go back to the origin of movements: being purer at their sources, they present an image still untainted. But readers who have come this far will remember that Boulangism was not a foundling, it was one incarnation of a political temperament that had found its name and personality in Bonapartism. To render the proof more convincing, we shall submit Gaullism to a comparison with Bonapartism, such as its second appearance, that of the Second Empire, finally developed it. The parallel with Boulangism must necessarily be limited: the latter scarcely lasted more than three years and was unable to emerge from the opposition; Gaullism on the contrary passed from the opposition to win power, as did Bonapartism. In consequence, the analogies stand out more readily between their methods of government and their policies. When the Fifth Republic's Minister of the Interior encourages the prefects not to remain neutral in politics, how can we keep from thinking of the political activity of the Imperial prefects and of the recommendations that they received from Persigny? Is not the present government prone to use the monopoly that the law gives it over television in the same way the Imperial regime acted toward the press a hundred years ago? The two regimes reassured the property owners, satisfying the desire for public order and the need for stability; they seemed to provide safeguards against nineteenth century Radicalism and twentieth century Communism.

They are not, for all this, purely reactionary regimes, they should not be identified with the unchanging maintenance of the status quo.

From René Rémond, *The Right Wing in France from 1815 to de Gaulle*, tr. James M. Laux (2nd American edition; Philadelphia, 1969). Reprinted by permission of the University of Pennsylvania Press.

They proclaim a concern for social issues; they interest themselves in labor problems and in workers' conditions; they abrogate regulations making strikes illegal or encourage a closer association between capital and labor by profit sharing or even by labor representation in management; and they find friends and guarantors among labor's elite. While Napoleon III had his cousin Prince Jérôme, General de Gaulle has the Democratic Union of Labor (U.D.T.), Léo Hamon, and Louis Vallon.* Their economic policies in particular are related, and this is one of the areas where they moved furthest away from the liberal Right. They used their authority to carry out reforms; they launched innovations. Among the Saint-Simonians of 1860 and the technocrats of 1960 there is the same confidence in autocratic initiative, the same desire to break the cake of custom and to ignore obstacles. This reformism is an essential component and prevents us from reducing this tendency to the conservative Right. Its union with stability perhaps is the most acceptable definition of this political phenomenon and the key to its success with the public. Yesterday's Bonapartism and today's Gaullism reconcile order and progress in the eyes of their voters; or to borrow a phrase from General de Gaulle himself, in which he summed up his program since 1945, the new and the sensible.

Once in power the two regimes preferred to resort to men with no political past, using the services of big businessmen, of high-level civil servants, of technicians or men who appeared to be such. The Baroches and Rouhers have their counterparts under the Fifth Republic.

The parallel even extends into areas where one might not have expected it. Does not Louis-Napoleon's policy of an Arab kingdom foreshadow in a way the Algerian policy of General de Gaulle, when he still envisaged some kind of association between the two countries? His decolonization policy, although it resulted in freeing some of the territories that the Second Empire had made into colonial dependencies, did not differ so much from it in its philosophy. And foreign policy? It presents material for some very interesting comparisons: in its formation the same secretiveness surrounding the key decisions; if the term "reserved area" had not been invented for

---

* The U.D.T. is a Left Wing Gaullist political organization, with Hamon and Vallon among its leaders.—Tr.

use in the Fifth Republic,* it might very well have been imagined for the Second Empire. The policy of encouraging all nations to achieve their independence and supporting the countries of the Third World against the imperialism of the great powers may well recall Napoleon III's policy of nationalities which aided young Italy against Austria.

We shall stop the parallel at this point, even though there is material to extend it further. Tempting as it may be, this is a dangerous exercise. Historical comparisons ordinarily are only the most subtle form of anachronism, and the highest virtue of historical intelligence is to know how to detect differences. Therefore we want to be clearly understood: it is not our hidden motive to show that Napoleon III continues to govern France behind the person of General de Gaulle and that the Fifth Republic is the restoration of the Second Empire. We shall leave these oversimplifications to the polemicists. Too many differences separate the two experiences— that between the Heads of State being an essential and decisive one in a regime of a personal type. In a century France also has changed too much in its political life as in its social situation for these changes not to have had some effect on institutions. The political support also is different. The Second Empire found its most faithful supporters in the countryside, while it is in the cities and regions of economic growth that the R.P.F. and then the U.N.R. have won their most solid successes. The two regimes are differentiated finally by their evolution. Bearing in mind the 1958 Constitution and the circumstances in which it was written, one might almost assert that the Fifth Republic began where the Second Empire ended.

But the quantity of similarities between the two movements, some superficial and others more fundamental, constitutes a presumption too strong not to accept the invitation to penetrate further into what shapes the essence of their political traditions, their basic principles, and their fundamental postulates.

Now, when distilled through the refinery of ideological analysis, to what elements can the essence of Gaullism be reduced? A passion for the grandeur of France, a yearning for national unity desired

* A reference to the provisions in the Constitution of the Fifth Republic which restrict the parliament's legislative power to certain areas and reserves others to the executive.—Tr.

for its own sake as much as a precondition for grandeur, and direct democracy. If one turns back to our presentation of Bonapartism the concordance cannot fail to be impressive, especially if one notices that the same elements take the first place in the scale of values. At once the similarities appear for what they really are, the symbol and result of a real kinship of inspiration. It is in the logic of the two systems to find support among the people consulted as a mass rather than through representative assemblies. As with Bonapartism, Gaullism incarnates a certain idea of direct democracy as expressed by means of the referendum. In some ways it achieves that mixture of authority and democracy, of appeals to the masses and anti-parliamentarism, which is so characteristic of the authoritarian Right. Yet it is to go too far to speak of the Right, for it is in the very nature of this tradition to try to avoid the dualistic framework. We cannot insist too much on the impossibility of reducing Gaullism purely and simply to the Right Wing, whether it be liberal, conservative, or reactionary. Actually, it is the very ambiguity of Gaullism, our difficulty in pinning it down, and the diversity of aspects that it presents (extending from a social Gaullism through a gamut of variants to one quite authoritarian), that certifies its relationship to the tradition. The same thing can be said of Bonapartism. Allowing for differences of persons, period, and circumstances, in our view Gaullism is the contemporary version of the tradition which, on its first appearance in France, assumed the countenance of Bonapartism, a Bonapartism that has been filtered and adapted, and those faithful to the Appeal to the People of the 1870s perhaps would consider quite changed. But it is the nature of traditions to evolve; indeed, what remains today of the initial monarchism of the most loyal and traditionalist of the Right Wing traditions? It is only at the price of these transformations that they can endure. Gaullism has interpreted, amended, and corrected; still it has kept the essence, the alliance of democracy and nationalism. By emphasizing as it does the deep-rooted approval of the country, by patting itself on the back for having given the people back its voice, by expanding the practice of democracy through the referendum and the election of the President of the Republic by universal suffrage, it has even brought the Bonapartist tradition back to its origins. After the Boulangist crisis the inordinate growth of the nationalist strain at the expense of the other components had accelerated the movement of nationalistic sentiment to the Right. Nothing remained any more of the democratic aspects that had been associated continuously with it since the Revolution. Now Gaullism tends to reconcile them. Perhaps this is a hidden, but decisive, cause for the implacable opposition to Gaullism by the extreme Right which had used nationalism for the profit of a counter-revolutionary ideology that was totally inconsistent with nationalism's democratic origins.

What has just been said refers to the essence of Gaullism and to its ideology. Actual practice often corresponds only distantly to it. Not only does Gaullism assume many forms, but reality pulls it in other directions. It has even succeeded in bending Gaullism toward a course that is somewhat parliamentary. Without being overly schematic, we can say that just like the Second Empire it fluctuates between the Bonapartist and Orleanist traditions. Also, in this double and contradictory attraction there may be a presentment of a mysterious law whose power extends not only over Gaullism but in addition governs all the Right Wing and perhaps by extension or by analogy, all French political life.

Suggestions for Additional Reading

The following list of suggested readings in no way represents, nor is it intended to be, an extensive, much less an exhaustive bibliography. Its sole intent is to serve as a guide for those readers who will want to round out their knowledge and deepen their understanding of Napoleon III and his times.

The best and most recent short introduction to the historiography of the Second Empire is Alan B. Spitzer's article "The Good Napoleon III," *French Historical Studies,* II, No. 3 (Spring, 1962). Robert Schnerb's older "Napoleon III and the Second French Empire," *Journal of Modern History,* VIII (Sept., 1936), is still useful. "The Varieties of History, 1814–1870," chapter 17 of Gordon Wright, *France in Modern Times* (Chicago, 1960), contains a neat summary of the historical debate over Napoleon III. The *American Historical Association's Guide to Historical Literature* (New York, 1961), and Jacques Droz, *et al., L'Epoque contemporaine: I. Restaurations et révolutions* (1815–1871) (*Collection Clio,* IX) (Paris, 1953), are convenient bibliographic tools.

There are a number of older works the importance of which lies less in the author's point of view than in the amount and type of information they contain. Pierre de La Gorce's aforementioned *Histoire du Second Empire* (7 vols., Paris, 1894–1905) remains the standard work in the field. Blanchard Jerrold, *The Life of Napoleon III* (4 vols., London, 1874–1882) is based on documents provided by the Imperial family. Octave Aubry, *Le Second Empire* (2 vols., Paris, 1938), also available in translation as *The Second Empire* (Philadelphia & New York, 1940), gives a comprehensive and balanced account of the reign. Emile Ollivier's massive apologia, *L'Empire libéral, Études, Récits, Souvenirs* (17 vols., Paris, 1895–1915), contains a wealth of useful material.

Taxile Delord, *Histoire du Second Empire* (6 vols., Paris, 1869–1875) stands out among the early critical accounts of the Second Empire for the length and violence of its indictment. Written in 1852 and first published in 1877, Victor Hugo's account of the coup d'état, *Histoire d'un crime,* is a companion piece to *Napoléon le Petit.* These two titles are readily available, both in French and English, in the many editions of the great poet's collected works. Albert Thomas, *Le Second Empire* (Jean Jaurès ed., *Histoire Socialiste,* X) (Paris,

1906), is a critical survey from the Socialist viewpoint. Albert Thomas also wrote "Napoleon III and the Period of Personal Government (1852–1859)," and "The Liberal Empire (1859–1870)," two chapters in volume XI of *The Cambridge Modern History* (London & New York, 1909). Charles Seignobos' account of the last years of the reign, *Le Déclin de l'Empire et l'établissement de La Troisième République* (Ernest Lavisse ed., *Histoire de France contemporaine,* VII) (Paris, 1921), adds up to a dispassionate but negative verdict. Another scholarly but unfavorable treatment is Henri Hauser, Jean Maurain, and Pierre Benaerts, *Du libéralisme à l'impérialisme (1860–1878) (Peuples et Civilizations,* XVII) (Paris, 1939).

The revisionist literature is extensive and growing. *The Rise of Louis Napoleon* (London, 1909) and *Louis Napoleon and the Recovery of France* (London, 1923), F. A. Simpson's pioneering studies, have already been mentioned. These two works deserve the attention of anyone who would study the Second Empire seriously. Robert Sencourt, *Napoleon III: The Modern Emperor* (London & New York, 1933) is another earlier English attempt at rehabilitation. Paul Guériot, *Napoléon III* (2 vols., Paris, 1933) still represents the best and most effective defense of Napoleon III by a French historian. Albert Guérard, *Napoleon III: A Great Life in Brief* (New York, 1955) is a short and highly readable restatement of this leading revisionist's thesis. Roger L. Williams' article "Louis Napoleon: A Tragedy of Good Intentions," *History Today,* IV (April, 1954), immediately placed him among the more forceful champions of Napoleon III in the United States. His *Gaslight and Shadow* (New York, 1957), a series of vignettes of some of the reign's leading personalities in many walks of life, represents a bold but effective approach to serious historical writing. This work is now available as a Collier Books paperback under the title *The World of Napoleon III, 1851–1870* (New York, 1962).

Two complementary studies on the nature of the regime are: Howard C. Payne, *The Police State of Louis-Napoleon Bonaparte 1851–1860* (Seattle, 1966) and Theodore Zeldin, *Emile Ollivier and the Liberal Empire of Napoleon III* (Oxford, 1963).

The social and economic aspects of the Second Empire have had special attraction for historians. General surveys like Shepard B. Clough, *France: A History of National Economics, 1789–1939,* Henri Sée, *Histoire économique de la France* (2nd. ed., 2 vols., Paris, 1951), and Rondo E. Cameron, *France and the Economic Development of Europe, 1800–1914: Conquests of Peace and Seeds of War* (Princeton, 1961) contain much valuable material on the period 1851–1870. Two excellent monographs on the Emperor's public works program are Louis Girard, *La Politique des travaux publics du Second Empire* (Paris, 1952) and David Pinkney, *Napoleon III and the Rebuilding of Paris* (Princeton, 1958). Georges Duveau, *La Vie ouvrière en France sous le Second Empire* (Paris, 1946) is a first-rate study of working-class conditions. In a lighter vein, but informative for all that, is Maurice Allem, *La Vie quotidienne sous le Second Empire* (Paris, 1948). The debate over the socio-economic policies of Napoleon III has been less acrimonious and the range of differing opinions somewhat narrower—especially of late.

The Emperor's foreign policy, however, has remained a much more controversial topic. Arthur William Kinglake, *The Invasion of the Crimea: Its Origin and an account of Its Progress down to the Death of Lord Raglan* (6 vols., London, 1863–1880), was instrumental in conjuring up the image of Napoleon III as an inveterate schemer and disturber of the status quo. Robert C. Binkley, *Realism and Nationalism, 1852–1871* (William L. Langer ed., *The Rise of Modern Europe*, XVI) (New York, 1935), was an early proponent of the counter-thesis that Napoleon III was a "good" European. This same argument is taken up in all the revisionist works previously cited. More critical assessments will be found in A. J. P. Taylor, *The Struggle for the Mastery of Europe, 1848–1918* (Oxford, 1954) and René Albrecht-Carrié, *A Diplomatic History of Europe since the Congress of Vienna* (New York, 1958). The debate over the causation of the Franco-Prussian War has been especially heated. Emile Ollivier, *The Franco-Prussian War and Its Hidden Causes* (George Burnham Ives tr., Boston, 1912) defends the French position; and Hermann Oncken, *Napoleon III and the Rhine: The Origins of the War of 1870–1871* (Edwin H. Zeydel tr., New York, 1928) states the case for Germany. Later works on the subject are Lawrence D. Steefel, *Bismarck, the Hohenzollern Candidacy, and the Origins of the Franco-Prussian War of 1870* (Cambridge, Mass., 1962) and Willard Allen Fletcher, *The Mission of Vincent Benedetti to Berlin 1864–1870* (The Hague, 1965). Michael Howard, *The Franco-Prussian War: The German Invasion of France* (New York, 1961) is an excellent account of the conflict itself.

The leading personalities of the Second Empire have attracted the attention of biographers. The following studies are especially useful: Harold Kurtz, *The Empress Eugenie, 1826–1920* (Boston, 1964), Rosalynd Pflaum, *The Emperor's Talisman: The Life of the Duc de Morny* (New York, 1968), Maurice Parturier, *Morny et son temps* (Paris, 1969), Robert Schnerb, *Rouher et le Second Empire* (Paris, 1949), and Noel Blayau, *Billault, ministre de Napoléon III* (Paris, 1969).

Finally, there are short but comprehensive treatments which provide the reader with handy, overall assessments of the Second Empire. Georges Pradalié, *Le Second Empire* (Collection *Que-sais-je?*) (Paris, 1957) ranks with Paul Blanchard, *Le Second Empire* (2nd. ed., Paris, 1956) among the best and most impartial brief French syntheses. In English, Brison Gooch, *The Reign of Napoleon III* (Chicago, 1969), J. P. T. Bury, *Napoleon III and the Second Empire* (New York, 1964), and "The Imperial Experiment, 1852–1870," chapter 12 of Gordon Wright, *France in Modern Times* (Chicago, 1960), are especially recommended. "The Second Empire in France," Paul Farmer's contribution to volume 10 of *The New Cambridge Modern History* (Cambridge, 1960) is a balanced account. The contrast between Farmer's assessment and the tone of Albert Thomas' chapters in the old *Cambridge Modern History* is in itself symptomatic of the road travelled in the historiography of the Second Empire during the last sixty years.